VISUAL NOTE-TAKING FOR EDUCATORS

VISUAL NOTE-TAKING FOR EDUCATORS

A Teacher's Guide to Student Creativity

WENDI PILLARS

W.W. NORTON & COMPANY
New York • London

For information about permission to reproduce selections from this book,
write to Permissions, W. W. Norton & Company, Inc., 500 Fifth Avenue, New York, NY 10110

For information about special discounts for bulk purchases, please contact
W. W. Norton Special Sales at specialsales@wwnorton.com or 800-233-4830

Manufacturing by Edwards Brothers Malloy
Book design by Bytheway Publishing Services
Production manager: Chris Critelli

ISBN: 978-0-393-70845-5 (pbk.)

W. W. Norton & Company, Inc., 500 Fifth Avenue, New York, N.Y. 10110
www.wwnorton.com

W. W. Norton & Company Ltd., Castle House, 75/76 Wells Street, London W1T 3QT

1 2 3 4 5 6 7 8 9 0

For Ian:
Create, play, learn, and explore, as you make each day
your own masterpiece . . . Always.

Mom and Dad:
Wilbur Wright advised young people on how they might succeed in
life: "Pick out a good father and mother, and begin life in Ohio."
Check.
Thank you for all the beginnings you've provided,
along with your sacrifices, gifts, and patience.

For my English Language Learners,
past, current, and future:
Remember, it's precisely
when others say you can't, that you must.

CONTENTS

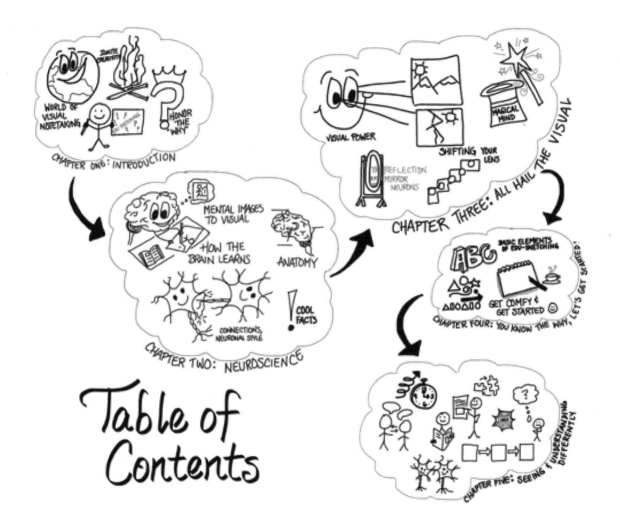

Table of Contents

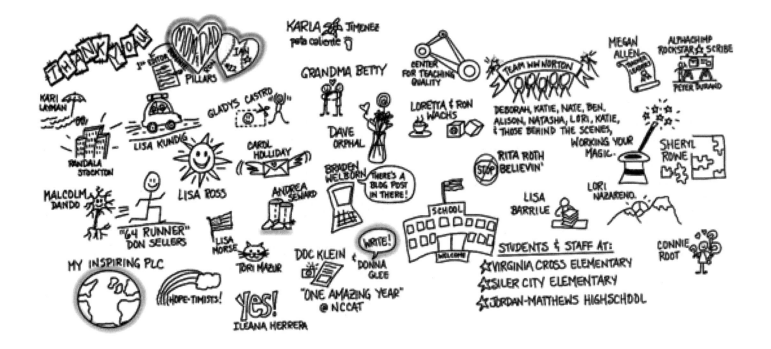

I've learned more than I could have dreamed along this book-writing journey, and if you know me, and we're in touch on any sort of regular basis, know that you have influenced me in some way. It's nearly impossible to acknowledge the cumulative influences at play, so forgive any inadvertent omissions. Thank you to the entire editorial staff at W. W. Norton for your guidance and patience. Special thanks to Deborah Malmud for taking a chance on me, and for that life-changing phone call nearly 2 years ago.

VISUAL NOTE-TAKING FOR EDUCATORS

Information from J. Medina (2008), *Brain Rules.*

A few years ago, I was absolutely mesmerized watching my first RSA Animate video.[1] Images were drawn as a story or talk was being narrated, and I found it tantalizing. I couldn't take my eyes off the screen. I was anticipating what the artist, Andrew Park,[2] would draw and how it related to what the narrator was saying, amazed at the visual representations he created and how he wrapped it all together so cleverly.

I wanted to do that. You see, as a teacher of English language learners, I've always sketched in class to quickly explain a vocabulary word, to break down difficult concepts, or to dispel misunderstandings. The kids always laugh at my silly drawings, but, hey, the information sticks better, and learning is a lot more fun. Sure, I've always encouraged my students to draw, too, but it wasn't until recently that I wondered how I could build more intentionally upon the joy I witnessed in them as they watched me sketch.

I decided to learn more about the RSA animated videos that captivated me so, and discovered visual note-taking—taking notes with words and images combined (also known as graphic visualization or sketchnoting). Initially, I learned about the work done by folks like Mike Rohde, Sunni Brown, Austin Kleon, and Brandy Agerbeck. As I did, I became more intentional about my own visual note-taking. I practiced at home, and began building my own visual library, a creative activity that keeps me thinking about the best ways to represent ideas in the curriculum and education.

I was not a sketcher in my school years. If you could see my notes from high school and college, they were copious, linear, and oh-so-detailed—yeah, I was "that nerd" who was the go-to note person—but never, ever would you find so much as a doodle or picture in my notes unless it was a specific diagram that I copied from the board. I never thought about expressing ideas visually or mixing words and images for my notes. Never.

Although I have sketched with my language learners since day one, it wasn't until a couple of years ago, well into my K–12 teaching career, that I finally began a journey with my students as we experimented with different ways of taking visual notes. I became more confident in my own abilities as I learned how to suppress my introvert fears of going public, and how much fun it was to share my visual notes with folks at conferences and meetings. I learned how to capture the bigger ideas visually and let go of my need to remember every single detail. And—incredibly—I physically felt the strain of a

---

1 The RSA (Royal Society for the encouragement of Arts, Manufactures and Commerce): "an enlightenment organisation committed to finding innovative practical solutions to today's social challenges. Through its ideas, research and 27,000-strong Fellowship it seeks to understand and enhance human capability so we can close the gap between today's reality and people's hopes for a better world. RSA Animates have revolutionised the field of knowledge visualisation whilst spreading the most important ideas of our time." RSA, accessed July, 2014, http://www.thersa.org/events/rsaanimate.

2 Creator of RSA Animate original concept and style. "Andrew_Park_(animator)," Wikipedia, http://en.wikipedia.org/wiki/Andrew_Park_(animator).

mental workout after an hour of intense listening and sketching during a talk. I was hooked. There was serious thinking going on.

I wanted my students to feel the same exhilaration and mental boost that I did. Sure, I could sketch concepts in advance of class. It would be expedient—and more polished.

But instead, I started drawing in class more frequently: sketching while we were reading complex ideas and sequences out loud, while we were learning vocabulary or predicting alternative endings. I even built these "visual moments" into bigger sketches in front of the kids. Near-instant synthesis! My kids were gloriously engaged and interested.

There was just one problem: I was learning more than my students. They needed to draw, too. It would be crazy not to share this with the thirsty brains of my kids. Although there's been some trial and error, I believe that increasing the visual powers of our students is a lifelong gift and is worth the efforts. Now, I'm not an artist or an art teacher, and I'm still learning—a lot—but my students have joined me and we are having fun along the way. My goal is to share the what, the why, and the how so you and your students can experience the same.

In this book, you will discover how to take notes differently, ways to optimize visual sketches in your classroom, and learn how they can transform your thinking alongside that of your students. There's a bit of neuroscience to boot, presented in a way that you can share with your learners, too.

I'm a fan of visual note-taking. Known by many other names such as graphic visualization, visible thinking, vivid thinking, visual record-ing, visual note-taking, scribing, even sketchnoting—it means quickly sketched images accompanied by phrases or key words.[3] Or it can be more linear notes accompanied by clarifying images. Either way, words and images used in tandem capture the essence of what is being said, discussed, or sometimes even read. What results is an engrossing interplay of text and images and some seriously satisfying thinking.

But wait. It's time to coin a new word, since this book now applies to you, dear educator-sketchers: that word is **edu-sketchers**. Those of you who use sketching as an intentional clarifying tool, to enhance understanding, or an alternative strategy for capturing learning, are edu-sketchers. Let's take a look at what's ahead for you and your students.

Chapter 1 explores the world of visual note-taking, busts a few myths, and ignites a little creative flame you barely knew existed. You'll get to be a learner again and bring your own perspective to illuminate what resonates most to you as we dig deeper into visual literacy. This chapter defines edu-sketching, provides examples, and

---

3 Graphic facilitators and visual facilitators are the folks who sketch at conferences and meetings of all shapes and sizes. They draw during conversations, problem-solving sessions, and solutions-oriented gatherings for businesses, nonprofits, and so on. These note-takers draw on large boards, papers, or canvases, so that everyone can see, share common meanings, and refine takeaways. The goals of graphic facilitating are to help lead—facilitate—folks to find solutions, whatever ilk they may be, with graphics to clarify and acknowledge input. This type of job requires multitasking and serious people skills, since the facilitators are drawing and engaging purposefully with the audience at once.

informs reasoning behind why you will want to try this in your classroom. You will understand why your brain is hooked on visuals and how using edu-sketching is not going to be something completely new for you—you'll get to see how you already use it in your classroom, then take it a step further.

Chapter 2 honors the neuroscience behind converting mental imagery to visual imagery, combining words and images, and learning in general. Our brains are fascinating, and you will realize just how much we take for granted in the learning processes of ourselves and our students. You may even experience neuroplasticity in its finest form as your brain learns new skills quickly, rewiring neural connections as you change your habits of thought and start to become a more visual thinker—and communicator.[4]

Chapter 3 examines some benefits of seeing things differently. We will build on some of the marvels of our thinking from Chapter 2. You'll think in metaphors, view content through a new lens, and learn about the powers of the visual mind and ways to be more intentional about using your own and awakening your students'. You will wonder why you've taken your powers of visualization for granted all these years.

Chapter 4 is all about getting started with visual note-taking. Edu-sketching was making me think differently, but we all want our students to experience that cognitive stretch, too. This entire book,

but especially Chapters 4 and 5, work best with actual practice. Reading them will give you ideas, but sketching your thoughts anywhere and everywhere on these pages will help cement the ideas behind the process and allow you to feel the mental challenge firsthand. The margins are fair game, as are the blank pages at the end of each chapter for your notes. As you will see in Chapter 2, the brain is much more efficient when it has chances to practice and play.

Chapter 5 is like a treasure chest of lightbulbs—full of ideas. You will see how retrieval and consolidation of information improve with edu-sketching, and connections become easier to create when you unleash the powers of your visual mind. This chapter gives lots of examples and ideas for you to steal, tweak, and otherwise manipulate for use with your own students and classroom. The ideas in this chapter are mere suggestions, but you will also find student samples from elementary and high school students alike, as well as examples of how I use them in class.

---

4 W. Pillars, "What Neuroscience Tells Us About Deepening Learning," *Education Week*, Teacher Edition, March 27, 2012, http://www.edweek.org/tm/articles/2012/03/27/tln_pillars_neuroscience.html.

CHAPTER ONE

What Is Visual Note-Taking?

Change your language and you change your thoughts.

—*Karl Albrecht*

You're a teacher. An educator and brain-changer in the ultimate sense of the term. This is what you do.

But you're frustrated. How, you wonder, do I enhance the memory and learning of my students? I'm repeating the same information time and again, and they still aren't making connections among all the bits of information. How can I grab and hold the attention of the kids in front of me? How can I better communicate the information I need to? I'm not engaging them consistently with their thinking and emotions. In my frustration, I'm neglecting the development of their skills—listening, visual, kinesthetic, and symbolic—and the connections among them as they navigate information.

Your students are your market and, in essence, you're not reaching them. They just aren't getting it. Note-taking is *boring*. Painful. The short track to hell. You name it, they've thought it or, more viscerally, felt it. Science and research, and—wait—skip all that.

Think about your own experiences. Think of the last PowerPoint presentation you experienced, or the last professional developer to show up at your school, rolling luggage in tow. From those presentation experiences, recall the following: how the information was relevant to you, how you implemented what you learned, and how you shared what you learned with others.

Now, think about your students. How often have they experienced the same lack of engagement, relevance, and opportunity to share what they're learning?

Too often, right? As an educator, though, having a bad day does not equate to being a bad teacher, so we reflect and seek new ways of reaching and engaging our students. Visual note-taking or sketching is one such strategy I, as a K–12 educator, use with my students. As you read this book, you will imagine and be able to apply many ideas of your own for this type of note-taking, which combines words with nonlinguistic representations, or images.

Along the way, even your own thinking will morph as you learn to view the world and your content through an edu-sketcher's lens: "I

I'd like to introduce Mnemosyne, "Momma of the Muses" and inspiration galore. Mnemosyne will accompany us on our journey throughout the book.

wonder how I could represent this concept visually to help my students understand." "I can't wait to see how students would visualize this idea—maybe this would be a good stopping point to synthesize this text so far." "Can my students represent the details of this text visually and connect them to the main idea?" "How will they demonstrate a connection from this information to what we read last month?"

If it sounds like a tall order, it's not. I have discovered wonderful insights into my students' thinking, thinking processes, and abilities—and have seen them enjoy far deeper understanding. And guess what? When their understanding is deeper, so is their engagement, which in turn makes it more relevant and easier for them to apply it to other situations.

Feel empowered rather than daunted as we begin this journey. You have the tools and the means to accomplish that hat trick of learning—engagement, relevance, and application—and enhance both encoding (the memory-stashing part) and recall for learners. Just be willing to give it a shot.

As you can see by these nonlinguistic symbols, meaning can be imparted quickly and clearly without a single word, and across linguistic barriers. Letters, on the other hand, are also merely symbols, yet we have created meaning from their combinations. How else can the letters b-a-t equate to an animal, a sporting tool and what you do with that tool, or a flirtatious action

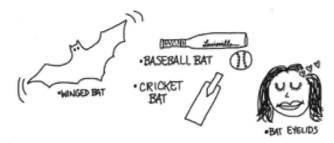

It fascinates me how one combination of three symbols (which we know as letters), can hold so many distinct meanings.

with your eyelashes? Someone created meanings out of those three symbols, then communicated those meanings to others—just as your students will do as they learn to edu-sketch.

Some research shows that 75% of our incoming information is processed visually.[1] That's some pretty savvy cognitive processing and as educators seeking ways of reaching our learners, we'd be crazy not to acknowledge it. Other research claims a lower percentage, but it's still much greater than the other senses: "the machinery that accomplishes these tasks is by far the most powerful and complex of the sensory systems. The retina . . . is actually an outgrowth of the brain . . . [and] neurons devoted to visual processing take up about 30% of the cortex" (as opposed to a mere 8% for touch and 3% for hearing).[2] Consider that each of the two optic nerves, which carry

---

1 D. Roam, *Blah, Blah, Blah: What to Do When Words Don't Work* (New York: Penguin, 2011).

2 Denise Grady, "The Vision Thing: Mainly in the Brain," *Discover Magazine*, June 1, 1993, http://discovermagazine.com/1993/jun/thevisionthingma227.

signals from the retina to the brain, consists of a million fibers, while each auditory nerve carries a mere 30,000.[3] Even though the exact numbers differ, what does remain the same throughout the research is an exponentially higher visual stake in working with incoming information.

In essence, when we think, we see, and we imagine. If we hear or read a word, an image comes to mind; it's so automatic that we don't pay attention to what is happening in our thinking. But we need to, and edu-sketching helps us do that.

Let's try a simple example: read the following word, then take about 2 minutes to sketch your mental image onto the page.

House.

I'm not going to say "I said so," but what just happened?

I didn't show you a picture to represent "house," but your mind's eye just kicked in.

What did your mind's eye conjure? A Spanish villa near the ocean? A log cabin in the snowy mountains? A thatched-roof hut in the rain forest? A famously obstinate doctor from a TV show of the same name?

When I gave this task to others, here are some images they sketched:

_____

3 Ibid.

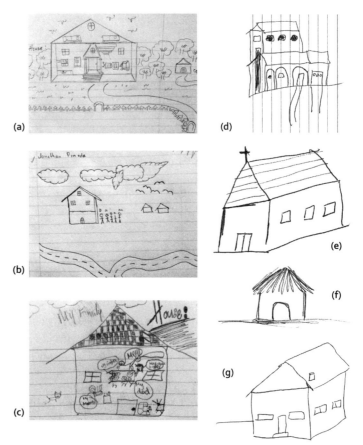

(a) (b) (c) (d) (e) (f) (g)

Notice the focus of "house" for the students (a,b,c) as compared to those of adults (d,e,f,g). What do you notice?

Here you can see—tangibly, visually—how the same word can conjure such a variety of images in our minds, and their subsequent conversions onto paper. The word "house" conjured up physical structures for some, whereas "family" was central to the thinking of others. If the seemingly simple concept "house" can have so many manifestations, imagine our students' thinking on a grander scale as they encounter our verbal information or written words in class. Imagery can be informed through culture, experience, and prior knowledge. Although each of our students may be receiving identical input from us, the brain's unique processing nearly assures nonidentical outcomes. Using visuals along with added verbal or written detail helps keep students in the same vein of understanding by providing a shared frame of reference. Having them create visuals based on their understanding will also provide you with valuable formative assessment information—within 2 minutes or less.

The 1990s were considered the decade of the brain. During and since that time, several myths about how the brain operates have been debunked. Yet there is a massive disconnect between the myths that have been uncovered and how we as educators have accessed the information, let alone applied it. I've also encountered other myths when I talk to people about sketching in class or show them my notes. What follows are just a few of the myths, a.k.a. "dangerous fear-mongering" thoughts, along with the newer thinking around them to refute your critical side and show you why these ideas are good for your classroom.

MYTHBUSTING

Myth 1: I'm not a visual thinker. I'm not creative!

This is the absolute first thing people tell me when I talk about my note-taking or they see some of it. It is now debunked. You are creative. It's your default thinking mode. Call it instinctual, but let's start thinking of it as invaluable. I am one of those people who believes everyone is creative; it's just not always manifested in the same way. One word ("house") just conjured up a picture in your head—that's creativity at work. Different than another's, perhaps, but a visual nonetheless. (Those differences, by the way, are what make edu-sketching so much fun—and so useful—in class.)

It's no coincidence that we use the phrase "the mind's eye" to refer to what we visualize and imagine within. Science has shown that the brain is what sees, not the eye.[4] It's also no coincidence that we use the phrase "I see" or "the bigger picture" to indicate understanding. As humans, we have a wonderful ability to visualize and imagine, to "see" something at will—whether in front of us or not, whether real or not, whether it has happened or not—and subsequently communicate it to others. Edu-sketching in the classroom is one such way of communication, and although not a panacea for all learners, it offers a pathway to understanding. Everyone, I daresay, has this potential, and it is potential that needs to be tapped in our students.

---

4 John Medina, *Brain Rules* (Seattle: Pear Press, 2008).

Myth 2: My students should all understand what I'm talking about. I explained it so well and used such precise words! They must not be very smart.

Also debunked. Words can only explain so much. As you saw with the example of "house," even the simplest concepts are not as simple as we assume them to be. The most basic words carry with them a whole host of meanings, both implicit and explicit, meanings that are derived from our experiences and prior knowledge, whether we realize it or not. Remember that the image in our heads about our content, despite our most honest intentions of clarity, will not always be the same image our students have.

Your imagined visual of a house just now was a confluence of all that is in your personal background and educational experience. Your brain integrated emotions and, most likely, other sensory input into your image—yes, maybe even the weather. (Was it sunny, cloudy, rainy, or something else in your mind?) Surrounding landscapes, maybe the neighborhood context? People involved or associated? I'm not saying your image was judgmental, but it was instantaneous—and nowhere near exactly like another person's image. Your image may have brought to light nuances that further compelled you to explain those details to someone else as you compared images. Had you limited yourself to a verbal description, the image in your listener's mind could be rather different.[5] How are you

building upon this knowledge of differences between your output and your students' interpretations in your teaching? How are you bringing to light the fact that so many connections are at play with what we consider even the simplest thinking?

Myth 3: Sketching is too much for my students to remember and do. I don't have time—I need to get through all of this content!

You're the adult here. You know there's a boatload of content, and then some, to get through. But it's worth your time to use images when you are teaching. Our brains are masters at remembering pictures. Studies show that when you hear a piece of information, you'll recall about 10% of it three days later.[6] If you add a picture to that information for your students, they'll be able to recall 65%.

Ten percent versus 65%? A 55% chance of increased recall just by using a picture? I'd say that's worth my time as an educator. It makes my job a whole lot easier, and a whole lot more interesting. This includes artwork, photographs, other primary sources, and edusketching to pull it all together. For instance, you might show students artwork of battlefields and photos of weaponry and General Gage, but then sketch out the expanse of events in Lexington and Concord as you talk about it. Besides lending geographical grounding, it also helps students understand a sequence of events.

---

5 We play a common game in the classroom when practicing vocabulary, speaking, and listening. One person draws a picture made of shapes, then directs the other students to draw the same thing. The trick is that the original artist can only use verbal commands, and cannot show the others the finished product until the end. Typically, the others' drawings are very different from the original, even though everyone heard the same directions, and the speaker was telling them exactly what he or she had drawn.

6 Medina, *Brain Rules*.

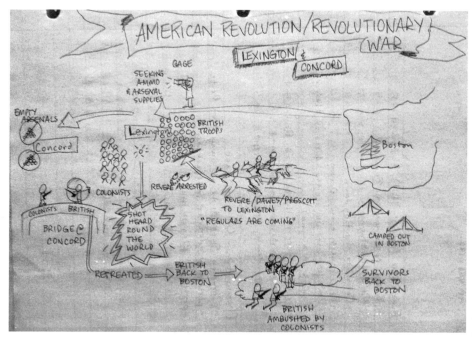

Don't just talk about it, sketch it out as you go!

intended it to be. If 75% of our thinking and understanding relies on the visual, it fails to make sense to continue our lecture-based monologues in class. We can no longer think it sufficient for our students to learn purely from the verbal when greater learning and understanding occur using visual support.

Keep in mind, too, that our average speaking rate is about 2.3 words per second, and a student's written note-taking ability hovers around .3 or .4 words per second. That's a whole lot of input without much time to filter and organize relevant information, which is unfortunate, since, as you will see in Chapter 2, this sorting and filtering process is where learning gets cemented. Despite the seeming inefficiency of handwritten note-taking, University of Washington research[7] suggests that physically writing notes activates regions of the brain that involve thinking, language, and working memory. Combining that with imagery solidifies the evidence to rethink what happens in our classrooms.

Armed with just these three debunked myths, let's rethink your classroom. We know that what we say and do creates images in our mind, on a consistent, if not continual, basis—we are visual thinkers by default. We also now know that what we think might be a simple concept may be interpreted by our students differently than we

It only makes sense to harness this visual prowess to make expla-

7 Maria Konnikova, June 2, 2014. What's Lost As Handwriting Fades. *New York Times.* http://www.nytimes.com/2014/06/03/science/whats-lost-as-handwriting-fades.html?_r=0

nations and ideas clearer, while acknowledging others' perspectives. Doing so engages your students more fully and allows them time to play with the information and deepen their understanding by sharing with others. Yes, it takes time at the beginning to introduce the concept and provide examples. When you have a paltry 80 days to whiz through world history, from the Paleolithic era to the present day, synthesis and critical thought are key. Edu-sketching can help students learn to capture the important points, make their notes far more interesting when they review and actively recall information, and also provide superb reference points when done together in class and displayed on the wall.

Mike Rohde, a master sketchnoter, reminds us that when "your mind and body act together, you can recall more of what you hear and draw."[8] Even if you're seated at your desk, your mind and body are more engaged while you are navigating your way through visual notes than if you were merely copying notes from the board, or listening to a 90-minute lecture. Giving students large pieces of paper to work on collaboratively at a table encourages all kinds of extended thinking, too—in conjunction with opportunities to get up and get moving.

So, there you have it. Three myths debunked. Here's the real scoop:

1. Everyone is a visual thinker because they create consistent images in their minds.
2. What you say is not precisely what others hear or understand, no

---

8 Mike Rohde, *Sketchnote Handbook* (San Francisco: Peachpit Press, 2013).

Notes from World History class about Mesopotamia.

matter how clearly you feel you are communicating. The brain brings much of its own stored knowledge to the table.

3. Time taken to introduce this note-taking strategy in class will actually save time and help your students understand how to break apart information into digestible chunks. This in turn will make your brain and its memory capacities much happier.

By engaging more intentionally with the information as they take time to synthesize and sketch, students are acknowledging what makes for a happy memory system: repeating to remember, and remembering to repeat.[9] As mentioned above, information thrown at us quickly disappears. Without information review, it takes just a few days to forget roughly 80% of what we originally learned.[10] Eighty percent. As in, only 20% remains. If that.

I believe that. I've witnessed it, as I'm sure many of you have, and it's disheartening for a teacher. Just ask your own children what they learned today, and their response sums up their learning in a depressing nutshell. "Nothing," they say. When kids rush out the door, intent on seeing their friends or getting to lunch, what will stick from your lesson? What would they remember? Why? Why not?

The Ebbinghaus curve, designed by Hermann Ebbinghaus, further demonstrates that information review is critical in order to retain it.[11] Memories can be refreshed through review (think of that first kiss—

or, equally exciting, the steps in mitosis) and a mere single review can reduce the steep forgetting curve. A few days after a single review, we will still remember about 40% of our information, as opposed to an anemic 20% with only the initial input phase.[12]

It's no wonder our learners so rapidly forget information. They're not doing it to make us question our sanity or our teaching. In fact, you can teach a wonderful lesson, but if it's meaningless information in the eyes of our learners, more than half of what you just taught will be lost a mere 20 minutes later.

20 minutes is enough time for students to lose half of what you just taught them.

Did I mention that was disheartening?

Well, hearten up. Rest assured that memories can be strengthened and refreshed through spaced and mindful review—both of which can be done handily through edu-sketching.

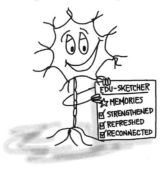

9 Medina, *Brain Rules.*

10 Klingberg, T., *The Learning Brain: Memory and Brain Development in Children* (New York: Oxford University Press, 2012).

11 Daniel L. Schacter, *The Seven Sins of Memory: How the Mind Forgets and Remembers* (Boston: Houghton Mifflin, 2001).

12 Ibid.

WHAT IS EDU-SKETCHING?

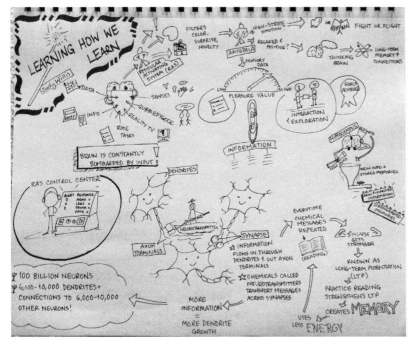

These notes were taken while reading the article "Learning How We Learn", by Judy Willis. Taking these notes forced me to think far more deeply about the processes of learning. Doing so makes unique cognitive demands in finding the connections and relationships among ideas. In the end, these notes were also far more effective as a review and reference tool than linear notes.

Yes.

Edu-sketching is visual note-taking.

But . . .

Edu-sketching is visual note-taking with intention, specifically geared for the classroom or the academic realm as another strategy to enhance learning, as another avenue to reach our students of all ages, mind-sets, and abilities.

Like visual note-taking, edu-sketching can be done publicly, for all to see and interpret what a speaker is saying, or it could just be for personal consumption, in a medium as small as a personal sketchbook or notebook. What matters most is the thinking process.

An additional bonus is that edu-sketching tools consist of pencil and paper—maybe markers and pens of various colors or possibly a tablet, but that's about it. That minimalism enhances the appeal of this thinking strategy, especially when multiple studies show that writing notes by hand is more effective cognitively than typing them on a laptop.[13] The value of taking notes lies in the

13 Denali Tjietjen, "Take Note of This: Handwritten Notes Are More Effective Than Typed Ones," Boston.com, June 5, 2014, http://www.boston.com/health/2014/06/05/take-note-this-handwritten-notes-are-more-effective-than-typed-ones/Ypp4ahKuX2Zd0O tUqBw79H/story.html; Robin Meyer, "To Remember a Lecture Bet-

extra time and deeper connections with the content as you reframe ideas in your own words—and now, images.

Sharing these notes fortifies confidence, relevance, and motivation when students begin to use each other's notes to further clarify and deepen understanding. Students can share out loud in groups or with a partner, and most certainly via social media. This type of note-taking generates a buzz that no linear notes ever will. I love bringing a sketchbook to conferences, but it wasn't until a couple of years ago that I started sharing my work at conferences personally and through social media as a thank-you to the speakers. I've even used them as an online teacher to help clarify lessons or capture online discussions. Sharing is always a dynamic community-building experience. Different speakers' and participants' ideas are validated in the notes when you use their thinking; participants can relive the talk or experience via the notes; and participants can also make new meaning of what is being said through a live note-taker's notes.

In class, it's exactly the same. Students love to add ideas to my drawings—kind of the Tom Sawyer mentality of painting the fence. Reluctance cedes to excitement, then they are bolstered to try it themselves because, frankly, it's pretty fun. Focusing on their sketches as they recall their learning also reduces the affective filter; it encourages kids to talk because they are looking at the sketch and not at others. Having an object of focus to talk about is an incredibly simple yet powerful language-learning strategy to encourage speaking.

ter, Take Notes by Hand," *The Atlantic*, May 1, 2014, http://www.theatlantic.com /technology/archive/2014/05/to-remember-a-lecture-better-take-notes-by -hand/361478/.

HOW DOES EDU-SKETCHING WORK?

Let's say you are reading a text, or listening to a speaker or teacher. You want to capture and remember the salient points, and so you take notes to review later. Throughout the process, though, images, connections, and thoughts about what you are hearing or reading are coloring your thinking. The visual imagery is nonstop. It's a mental New York City, open and active 24 hours a day. Edu-sketching captures that imagery and makes it tangible.

Mental imagery is nonstop!

WHAT IS VISUAL NOTE-TAKING?   **15**

If you ever tried to read without imagining what it all looks like, I think you can agree with my very nonscientific conclusion that it is nearly impossible. (I know there are always outliers.) So why do we suppress visual images? Why do we go the way of verbal, linear notes and dismiss pictures as immature, distracting, or too time-consuming in class?

Welcome to the ironic process theory, which postulates that when we are trying not to think of something, that's exactly what we will do—repeatedly, and sometimes to a point of obsession.[14] From the classic study of thought suppression where participants were asked not to think of a white bear or even a pink elephant, scientists have learned that trying to stop the brain from thinking certain things will more likely have the opposite effect.[15] You simply can't stop your brain's natural tendency to conjure a steady flow of imagery. Now we just need to embrace and optimize that tendency. By the way, don't think of a pink elephant. . . . Embrace and optimize your imagery.

Whether input is verbal or visual, it is widely accepted that unless you actually do something with that input, and the resultant imagery, or somehow connect it with information already nested in your long-term stores, your working memory will, in essence, reboot. Much of your learning will be lost.

Let's refresh what we know so far, because our aim is to be solution oriented here, rather than disheartened by the thought of too much lost learning.

- Our brains love practice.
- Brains need repetition and review because they have limits.
- Brains love, love, love visuals and imagery, yet they struggle with a still-evolving cranial skill set for reading.
- Brains, above all, as you will see in Chapter 2, need oxygen, which is best delivered through movement.
- Brains need connections and applications for what they learn.
- Brains need more repetition.

Why wouldn't we want to use a strategy like edu-sketching that is consistent with the way the human mind works?

WHY IS EDU-SKETCHING IMPORTANT FOR OUR CLASSROOMS?

As mentioned above, our brain is wired to be visual, to think visually, and to process information and ideas in pictures. Edu-sketching is a process of transferring those pictures and movies in our heads onto paper using nonlinguistic representations in the classroom. (Nonlinguistic simply means pictures, or nonverbal means of communication.)

---

14 Daniel M. Wegner, David J. Schneider, Samuel R. Carter III, and Teri L. White, "Paradoxical Effects of Thought Suppression," *Journal of Personality and Social Psychology* 53, no. 1 (1987): 5–13; David J. Schneider, "The White Bear Story," *Psychological Inquiry* 14, no. 3/4 (2003): 326–329.

15 Wegner et al., "Paradoxical Effects of Thought Suppression"; George Lakoff, *Don't Think of an Elephant! How Democrats and Progressives Can Win: Know Your Values and Frame the Debate: The Essential Guide for Progressives* (White River Junction, VT: Chelsea Green, 2005).

- EXCITED TO SHARE
- SELF-CONFIDENCE
- PRESENTER
- ENTERTAINER
- ORAL PRESENTATION

- FUTURE
- HOPE
- DREAMS
- COLLABORATION
- TEAMWORK
- DREAMWORK
- GOAL
- SUCCESS
- SURPRISE

Learning transfer is what makes our learners shine.

symbols might be sufficient without any words. And since note-takers are listening actively, or reading with intent, it becomes far more than just drawing pictures and more akin to an actual visual language since we are translating and combining ideas. A cognitive mash-up, if you will.

Nearly two decades ago, Robert Horn touted the complexity inherent in images: "Visual language communication units are both more demanding for readers and more immediately comprehensible. Because multiple levels of visuals, text, and concepts are combined, they require readers to spend a little more time in synthesis in order to come away with the full meaning of the communication. At the same time, the presence of familiar visual images provides a point of immediate entry and understanding that often bypasses linear apprehension."[16]

In essence, both viewers and creators of visual language communicate through simpler images that belie the complexity of thought required. And that deeper involvement with the content, the extra time it takes to uncover that full meaning, is where the sweet spot of learning lies.

Allan Paivio's dual coding theory proposed that "recall and recognition is enhanced by presenting information in both visual and verbal form."[17] Multimedia expert Richard Mayer agrees, saying the

In essence, edu-sketching makes our students' learning both visible and tangible, on paper, with nothing fancier than a pencil or pen. Students transform an abstract mental image into a concrete visual image—translating a dialect of their subconscious into pictures along with key words from the original text or speech to take notes. They can be public or private, with lots of words, or just a few. Some

---

16 Robert Horn, *Visual Language: Global Communication for the 21st Century* (New York: MacroVU Press, 1998).

17 M. Hardiman, *Connecting Brain Research with Effective Teaching: The Brain-Targeted Teaching Model* (Lanham, MD: R&L Education, 2003); "Dual Coding Theory (Allan Paivio)," Instructional Design, accessed July 2014, http://www.instructionaldesign.org/theories/dual-coding.html.

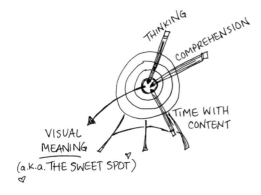

best way to foster learning involves both words and pictures.[18] Ideal learning makes use of an image or piece of realia (visual route) while someone describes, explains, or talks about it (auditory route). Many studies have addressed multiple areas of intelligence, although the trend is now toward tapping into different learning styles, recognizing that most tasks require more than one intelligence and learning style working together.

There seems to be a much greater understanding that even at the single-word level, multiple brain areas are activated when stimulated. Renowned neuroscientist David Sousa reports, for example, that the more highly contextualized or concrete a word is, the more brain wave activity there is in the frontal lobe area.[19] The more abstract and decontextualized a given word, the more activity there is in the top (parietal lobe) and rear (occipital) areas of the brain. I find it fascinating to think that scientists can pinpoint with increasing clarity such specific areas of activation. What I find intriguing is that there isn't much chatter among the areas.

The lack of interaction led Sousa to assert that our brains separate verbal-based versus image-based information. What this means for us is that it's vital to use images not only for the concrete, but also for the more abstract concepts—another perfect entry for edu-sketching. For a 3-minute brain break, ask your learners how they would represent the concepts of justice, freedom, or evolution and see how they surprise you.

Try it yourself, and when determining how to represent these ideas, pay attention to how many ideas you briefly consider, then discard, before actually creating the sketch. In other words, how much information do you know, and how do you extract the most salient points? As you weigh previous knowledge with current information, comparing and contrasting what you know within the context of the word, you anxiously wonder if it's going to be correct. Much is involved. Drawing a sketch is neither simple nor easy for the mind, but that's why it craves the challenge. Try it here.

---

18 Richard Mayer, *Multimedia Learning*, 2nd ed. (New York: Cambridge University Press, 2009).

19 D. Sousa, *How the Brain Learns to Read* (Thousand Oaks, CA: Corwin, 2014).

In any case, it is clear that multiple modes of presenting information will span a variety of learning styles and preferences and maximize the brain's propensity for learning. Expanding our students' inventory of learning strategies does them a service, especially when combining and sifting through so much information is an increasing challenge. Edu-sketching may not be a strength for everyone, but it does demonstrate that you do not have to be a visual learner to benefit from visual language.

That's a lot to think about. Let's review.

Edu-sketching provides the opportunity for the learner to savor the moment, and allows students to reflect on what they are learning. This, in turn, optimizes their visual language capacity. Instead of feeling like you're nailing Jell-O to the walls of your classroom, this focus on creating visuals, then using them to help communicate what students have learned, helps make learning stick and becomes an unparalleled formative assessment.

Piecing information together is powerful.

You will notice that edu-sketching helps tap into students' active listening as they learn to hone in on connections to prior knowledge. Their simultaneous or interactive note-taking invites them to stay present as they listen to a talk. Examples of how to introduce edu-sketching and subsequently apply it abound in Chapter 5.

Despite our brain's strong penchant for visuals and making sense of imagery, edu-sketching will challenge your students, so expect some amount of resistance at first. It may be an entirely different way of thinking for many of your students, but remind them that the art of being attentive to the mind's imagery can be improved with practice (and yes, give them time).

EDU-SKETCHING IN MY CLASSROOM?

There is definitely a home for visual language in your classroom, no matter the age of your students or your content area. And yes, edu-sketching helps develop critical thinking skills—within both creator and interpreter, while satiating the creative muses that have been neglected for so long.

Visuals help that proverbial Jell-O stick!

Fear not: I am not—nor will I ever—tell words and your linguistic side to abandon ship.

Thinking like an edu-sketcher, you wonder? Are you wondering how things can be different? Here's just a peek at some of the ways your own thinking will change as you tap into the strengths of your students' thinking.

- You will start to wonder how information can be represented visually. More abstract concepts will push you to consider whether you want to sketch something first or let the students try their hand first. Trust that they are very capable of coming up with great ideas. I often rely on them when I am stuck.
- "This is a good place to have my students draw a quick sketch in the margins to demonstrate their comprehension" is a particularly valuable formative assessment for poetry comprehension with its bountiful figurative language. Think of places within the texts, regardless of genre, and quickly have them sketch the image in their mind at that point. This works especially well with my language learners, and for reining in student focus on the details of any text.
- "Hmmm. Wonder how we could sketch this process together to make it easier to understand." Draw while the students tell you what to draw. It's useful to stimulate their creativity, and also to demonstrate firsthand how their mental images inevitably differ from everyone else's, including yours.
- "Whoa. I get two pictures in my mind when I read this; I wonder what my kids will be thinking when they read it." An interesting stretch for you is to anticipate misconceptions or different ways the text may be interpreted from the perspective of the edu-sketchers themselves.

In this era of Common Core–influenced curricular shifts, edu-sketching also teaches us to let go of every tiny detail in favor of making connections between prior and new knowledge, and seeking the bigger picture. Edu-sketching is about the thinking process, not about the pretty, and you'll read that over and over in this book: process over pretty. Academically, that thinking and reframing process is exactly what we're aiming for. Conceptual representations reign. If pretty happens, then that's a bonus. Don't get me wrong; details do matter, but you will find that instead of focusing, for example, on the dates of every historical event, kids will start to connect some dots within the bigger picture. As they do, there will be a natural place for those dates within the sketches, or you may see the dates manifest themselves through the layout of the sketches themselves.

BUILD ON WHAT YOU AND YOUR STUDENTS ALREADY KNOW

Before you get anxious at the thought of incorporating yet another thing or something so new and possibly awkward, I want to remind you of all the ways you already use visualizing in your classroom. You remind your students to make pictures or a movie in their minds as they read or listen to you read. You ask students to draw sketches to differentiate among homonyms and homophones. Maybe you use sketches to assist language learners in their understanding, or use comic books to teach visual literacy.[20] You remind students to "show, not tell" when they are writing. You have students create visuals to represent new vocabulary words and concepts in science. Edu-sketching is the next logical step because it pulls it all together and emphasizes the reasons why.

Why do we do this? Because doing so lets instinct take over during what can be a taxing cognitive process. There's only so much our working memory can hold; encouraging our kids to use graphic organizers or to sketch out the pictures they have in their minds while writing, for example, can release a slew of pressures to remember every single step of the writing process on top of the content. Their audience is more likely to "see what the writer sees" (and see what the writer means), thereby enhancing their transfer of mental imagery and empowering their communication. Getting the basics down helps free the mind to focus on other details.

When you record what you are reading or hearing, you are connecting to knowledge you already have—your own perceptions, background knowledge, and interpretations of what the speaker is saying. I personally see that as a bonus, and you can use that realization to your benefit to help deflect any note-taking pressures you or your students might feel. It is still, however, an intense listening, thinking, and information-synthesizing process, one that can literally transform your thinking process, as it has mine. Breaking down information into its most digestible bits in order to communicate it more effectively is your essence as an educator, right? You're not dumbing it down by any means, but you are providing serious foundational knowledge for your students, as well as teaching them how to do the same. Edu-sketching is one extraordinarily engaging strategy to help both you and your students maximize their learning.

Sunni Brown has done incredible work around doodling with a wide range of applications, from home to business to education, and her techniques on doodling, like edu-sketching, can be applied specifically to the classroom. Like edu-sketching, doodling shares the "deep and necessary information processing. . . connecting neurological pathways with previously disconnected pathways. . . sifting through information. . . and generating massive in-sights."[21] In short, drawing or sketching while listening, reading, or thinking helps us make those connections—with great cognitive rewards in recall and retention. But it also makes important demands on our listening and thinking.

Edu-sketchers need to be outstanding listeners and thinkers—far

---

20 Kevin Hodgson, "Teaching Literacy Skills with Quality Comics," Middle Web, June 17, 2014, http://www.middleweb.com/15846/teaching-literacy-with-comics/.

21 Sunni Brown, *The Doodle Revolution* (New York: Portfolio Hardcover, 2014).

more than to be "artists." Let me say that again: edu-sketchers need to be outstanding listeners and thinkers, more than focusing on the artistic quality of their work. Learning happens during the process of drawing, and this is what we need to emphasize to the students. What emerges with practice are clearer mental models that dispel confusion—and serve as quick formative assessments.

If you think you aren't an artist, we will try a few creativity exercises later to respectfully prove you are incorrect, dear edu-sketcher. (And you can then use similar introductory strategies with your students.) What is more

important than your inner da Vinci is the Process. My mantra for my students is the acronym POP, for the aforementioned "process over pretty." I tell them, "I need to know you get it, but I'm not worried

about how pretty your sketches are." As Brandy Agerbeck says, "Content is King."[22] If you aren't listening and getting the main idea, it doesn't matter how phenomenal your drawings look because the gist is missing.

Edu-sketching and quick visuals during read alouds, in the margins, with poetry, a historical passage, or excerpts from a chapter book, can demonstrate your students' linguistic access. Do the students understand the concept or word via context or are they relying solely on what they hear in a single word? Do they grasp the context, or the gist, but not details, or vice versa?

As you can "see," good listening has to happen on our part, too. If being an outstanding listener and thinker sounds daunting, let's consider the following.

The beauty of visual note-taking and your listening skills is that they can be strengthened and enhanced. Your lenses for seeing and connecting, along with your purposes for listening, will change. Your attunement to the world will also change. You will automatically begin connecting contextual dots where there were none before. You will begin wondering how you can represent concepts and ideas with a simple visual. Your brain will change. Yeah, it might hurt.

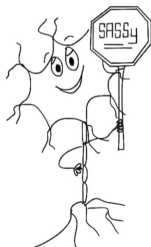

As mentioned before, your perspective on planning will change, too. You will start finding good stop-and-synthesize points (SASSy points, as I like to call them), ripe for visuals to consolidate learning. This will then help craft a bigger picture, and help ascertain ways to make more connections. You will also start sifting through your content information in new ways to ensure you've made the essence crystal clear. These are all learning strategies that make for happy

---

22 Brandy Agerbeck, *The Graphic Facilitators' Guide* (Loosetooth, 2012).

brains (a.k.a. "brain-compatible"), which we will learn more about in Chapter 3.

Other aspects of planning will requiring slightly tweaked pacing, since the hands-on nature of visual note-taking results in greater student engagement. Some of my most deeply struggling readers and writers shine when they get to create visuals, and it always reminds me to step back and remember this: our kids' minds are incredibly adept at making connections and understanding, even when they are unable to express themselves verbally. Which means, even if you're hesitant to try something new like edu-sketching in your classrooms, it may be just the key to unlock the knowledge of your less verbally inclined learners. I can just about guarantee that you will be fascinated by the differences in your students' mental imagery. It's one of my favorite reasons to use sketches in class.

For example, to teach the word "ancient," I gave a quick definition ("very very old" or "a very long time ago"), and asked the kids what we could use as a visual to represent that concept for "ancient stories." My favorite was one boy's use of cobwebs above and around a book. When I asked him to explain why he chose that image, thus incorporating the oral synthesis of his thinking, he told me, "Haunted houses have those spider-thingies, and those houses are very, very old and spooky." Although I didn't emphasize the aspect of "spooky," his connection was concrete enough so that his recall of that word was unhesitating months later.

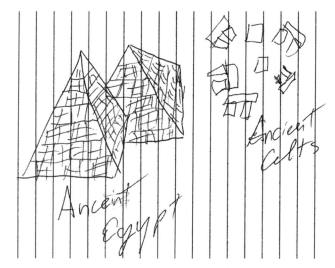

Which knowledge connections are activated and what are they based upon? Why do you think that is? What questions are you asking as you determine what to draw? What else do you need to know? How can you picture using this with your own students?

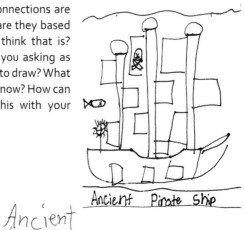

My older students also represented the word "ancient," but our context for the word was very different, and their sketches reflect that. Here are two other sketches by second graders: you can see right away the differences in what resonates with the kids, even though we learned the word at the same time. Pyramids, cobwebs, and pirates, oh my! (Isn't it fascinating?)

What the kids really liked about this was taking a quick break, a compellingly simple way to make a happy brain. Taking a break every 10–15 minutes (or at least every 20 minutes) can help consolidate learning: a 2-minute sketch enhances memory and recall exponentially. Try it yourself again. How would you represent the concept of "ancient"? What thoughts roll through your mind? Again, pay attention to which thoughts you keep and which you prune away.

If you're telling yourself that your class is exciting enough that your students don't need brain breaks, think again. If you think kids nodding off and being easily distracted by nonacademic material is their fault, think again. Chances are, if you're thinking those thoughts, you're also thinking, "I don't need brain breaks," or "my students got this."

There's such a thing in the education world as an attention span rule of thumb. An oft-accepted happy medium for attention span limits is age plus 2 minutes, on up to about 20 minutes for adults. So, my third graders, ages 7–9, would, according to this rule of thumb, enjoy 9–11 minutes of instructional time before they need some sort of break to consolidate what they just learned. My high schoolers would work 16–20 minutes before a break—critical in a 90-minute block! (Of course, those times depend on motivation, technology, topics, and all sorts of other factors.) Using sketches breaks up the routine, or enhances it—and can be used in all sorts of ways that we will talk about in Chapter 5. If you want to know more now, feel free to visit both Chapters 4 and 5 to find the resources.

Drawing in front of your kids, ahead of time, or even using previously drawn sketches so you can spend time with details, takes advantage of limited time in class and uses the sketches as a discussion launchpad. I've found time and again that my sketching helps my students understand how the people, the sequence, the vocabulary, and so on, support and bridge their thinking to overarching themes. This bridge is what helps our learners make sense of what can be an overload of information.

Patrick Henry may have said it best in 1799: "United we stand,

United, our thoughts stand, divided, they fade away.

divided we fall." Although historians attribute his quote within the context of the Kentucky and Virginia Resolutions, I can apply this same thinking to our wondrous thoughts. When thoughts connect, they are retained and understood more thoroughly, while those which are unconnected and decontextualized quickly fade away.

More ideas for implementation will come in Chapters 4 and 5. But first, let's explore the inner workings of the brain in Chapter 2. Although you may question why it's important, shift your lens. Suspend doubt, and let yourself be fascinated by how all of this learning stuff and visual imagery occur, down to the cellular level. I wish I had known this information before I started teaching, and even more so as a student. As an edu-sketcher, you are not only bringing a different learning strategy into play, but you are also in the perfect position to teach your students about the concrete physiological processes of learning.

That, dear colleagues, is something to imagine and visualize. Now make it tangible. The next chapter has the tools to get you started.

CHAPTER TWO

The Neuroscience of Visual Learning

Your brain contains roughly 100 billion nerve cells, 32 million kilometers of "wires," a million-billion connections, all packed into a volume of 1.5 litres, but weighing only 1.5 kg, and consuming a mere 10 watts—about the same amount of electric power as a night light. If we tried to build such a brain using silicon chips, it would consume about 10 megawatts, i.e., enough electricity to power a town. To make matters worse, the heat produced by such a silicon brain would cause it to melt.

—*British Neuroscience Association,* Neuroscience: Science of the Brain

Recent decades have been a particularly good time to be a brain. The Decade of the Brain from 1990 to 2000 promoted benefits derived from increased brain research, thanks to improved brain imaging.[1] It had a tremendous impact on the trove of information we now have about neuroscience and how the brain works, especially at the cellular level in learning and memory or even aging and cell death. Even as a curious educator with interests in science, I never learned about how the brain actually works, how memories are formed, or how intricate the unity is between structure, function, and origin until I had time to research on my own, well after my formal education.

Although scientists have learned exponentially more about the inner workings of the brain since this 1990s push, they acknowledge that this knowledge is a mere fraction of what there is yet to discover, know, and understand about the human brain.

These findings are not always accessible to us as educators, given time constraints—and perhaps motivational constraints. Learning what I have about the brain's nonlinear and complex processes has encouraged me to learn even more. More importantly, it has caused me to rethink how I teach, with greater understanding in how we learn and how we can make sure it happens with our students.

This chapter examines the brain's structure and functions to render the biological basis of learning more explicable. I first look at the general physical structure of the brain, including both its major components and its developmental basics. This is followed by a more in-depth look at neuronal activity, and how neural networks are formed that lead to functions of learning and memory. This knowledge provides the basis for Chapter 4, where the discussion turns to uses of edu-sketching in the classroom as a strategy to employ the countless powers of our brain networks.

The following information is not meant to replace scientific coursebooks, as I have no designs on becoming a scientist; rather, it presents an account of what happens in the brain from the viewpoint of a concerned teacher who feels the necessity to understand the brain's learning processes in order to maximize them. The information may be a review to some, or brand new to others; regardless, it

1 "Project on the Decade of the Brain," Library of Congress, accessed July 2014, http://www.loc.gov/loc/brain/.

is worthwhile to augment your knowledge with the recent findings about the learning processes of our brains. Remember that it is our brain that allows us to study the brain—with all of its inherent limitations. The recent findings in this age of neuroscience are fascinating, and we as educators can use them to explain basic neurobiology to our students, while becoming better consumers of the exhausting amounts of brain-based research. Perhaps your thinking will shift as you reconsider just how many cognitive intricacies are involved in reading and learning. It is nothing short of a miracle.

One of the most critical pieces of learning is learning it well enough to share with, or teach to, others. As we explore the biology of the brain and of learning, please think about the ways you can

- apply this knowledge with your students in the classroom;
- apply this knowledge in your planning;
- adopt strategies that align with neuroscientific findings (data-driven);
- and share this knowledge with your students and colleagues.

As you do so, you will find yourself asking questions, sparking curiosity in others, and tweaking your instruction to catalyze deeper learning. The simplest reason why is that now, more than ever, your focus is on student learning.

PREASSESSMENT QUESTIONS

An anticipation guide is a comprehension strategy teachers use before reading to activate students' prior knowledge while building up anticipation—or curiosity—about the topic at hand. Students respond to statements that may challenge common knowledge or support concepts that are already known. Revisiting these statements and ideas during or after reading promotes a purpose for reading and enhances student engagement. (And most certainly, sketches and images can be included in an anticipation guide to poke their inferencing skills.)

The following questions will be answered throughout your reading, but try answering them first to see how much you already know.

1. T / F   The brain accounts for only about 2% of your body's weight, yet it consumes 20% of the oxygen we breathe and gets about 20% of the blood flow in our bodies.
2. The average adult has approximately how many brain cells?
   a. 100 million
   b. 3 trillion
   c. 100 billion
3. T / F   The average adult has twice as many brain cells as a fetus does.
4. T / F   Neurons are nerve cells that work by sending electrochemical signals to and from the brain and nervous system.
5. T / F   Only about 50% of the brain's nerve cells are neurons.
6. Three major parts of the brain are the cerebrum, cerebellum, and the
   a. frontal lobe
   b. brain stem
   c. cerebral cortex
7. T / F   Brain cells fade away when neurons that don't receive or transmit information are damaged.

8. T / F The right hemisphere of the brain controls the left side of the body.

9. T / F The right hemisphere is purely responsible for holistic and artistic thinking, while the left hemisphere is responsible for analyzing and organizing.

10. T / F The average adult uses only 10% of his or her brain.

Bonus: What do these things have in common?

OUR AMAZING BRAIN

The brain is an organ weighing about 1.5 kilograms, consisting of billions of tiny nerve cells, with a mind-boggling intricacy and complexity of neural networks. The brain can perform countless functions, but its development depends on quite an array of external and internal influences. One of the brain's greatest ironies is that its efficiency precludes the necessity for us to even think about how it controls the

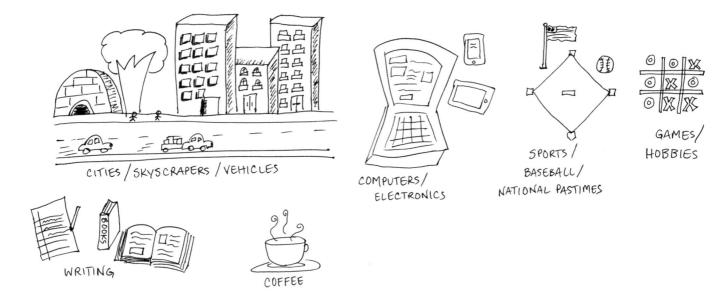

CITIES / SKYSCRAPERS / VEHICLES

COMPUTERS / ELECTRONICS

SPORTS / BASEBALL / NATIONAL PASTIMES

GAMES / HOBBIES

WRITING

COFFEE

very essence of our humanness. It provides us with our individuality and allows the body to function without any conscious responsibility for each breath, eye blink, emotion, and organ task. Imagine if we had to consciously do all of that. It is an amazing organ, which is more often than not taken for granted. Quite simply, the brain is the one organ that deserves its own superhero cape and can be considered the very foundation of our existence.

BRAIN-IMAGING TECHNIQUES

Before looking at the brain itself, it is helpful to briefly identify the sources of these findings. Understanding how the brain works has

come a long way since phrenologists attempted to gather knowledge by caressing bumps on the skull and, to many, such practice now seems outrageous. Immense research strides of recent decades —particularly the Decade of the Brain—have unquestionably challenged previous knowledge. Ironically, contemporary scientists have also gleaned their knowledge by examining the brain from outside the skull, albeit with modern brain-imaging techniques that let us peek inside. It is stunning to contemplate that technology gains in the past couple of decades have provided us with unprecedented levels of increasing clues and facts about the brain's inner workings. Yet at the same time, we as educators haven't been privy to the details without intentional efforts.

This knowledge concerning the brain's intricacies without the need for surgery, bump analysis, or, heaven forbid, trepanning, has occurred largely due to a handful of techniques developed within the past three to four decades: magnetic resonance imaging (MRI), functional MRI, positron emission tomography, near-infrared spectroscopy, electroencephalography, and magnetoencephalography (see Appendix A for more detailed descriptions of each of these techniques and the visions they provide to modern science). The central basis for each of these monitoring technologies is tracking changes in energy due to the oxidation of glucose, which is required to activate the monitors. Blood delivers both oxygen and glucose within the cerebrum, and the changes within this blood flow act as an index for neural activity.

Through analysis of these changes and their resultant neural activity, we now know how gluttonous the brain is in its energy consumption. The brain is your body's teenager with its monumental appetite for energy. It is a glucose-sucking, oxygen-bingeing, and toxic-waste-dumping machine. At a svelte 3 pounds, the brain may constitute a minute percentage (2%) of your overall body weight, but, energy glutton that it is, it consumes about 20% of your body's energy to operate and receives 20% of your body's blood flow. When the "brain is fully working, it uses more energy per unit of tissue weight than a fully exercising quadricep!"[2] To do that, it uses about 70% of your body's glucose, 25% of your body's oxygen,[3] about 8

gallons of blood per hour for its 100,000 miles of capillaries and blood vessels, along with about eight glasses of water per day (and here you thought that water was for the rest of your body).

Even more fascinating to consider is that if 2% of your neurons were to perform and fire at once, you'd faint from the exertion and the drain on your glucose supply.[4] So, on particularly intellectually taxing days, perhaps we should warn our students to bring a pillow. (I suppose that also explains the meaning behind "mental exhaustion.")

(Remember the "Warning" at the beginning of the book?)

Further analysis of these activities within our brain has shown the brain's patterns of blood flow, areas of activation during specific activities, and even changes in neural structure. Consider the images of neuroscience as maps of the brain's terrain that show us where to look if we want to know more about how the brain learns, thinks, remembers, dreams, or feels emotions. Current technology enables scientists and laymen alike to witness these activities and changes in real time.

BRAIN STRUCTURE

"One should keep in mind that the neuronal mechanisms came to us by the long evolutionary process of trial and error. For our nervous systems—for us—to learn and remember means that evolution not only had to learn and remember, but that it had to learn and remember how to learn and remember."[5]

Learning is the process through which we acquire new information, and memory is the process by which we keep, organize, and retrieve that information over time. This dual process is central to our humanness and to our individuality within a rapidly progressing society. It's time to explore the greater structure of the brain, to lay the foundation for understanding physical changes at the cellular level during the learning and memory processes.

Your brain, by the numbers:

2 John Medina, *Brain Rules* (Seattle: Pear Press, 2008), 20.

3 "Human Brain Statistics," Statistic Brain, accessed October 2014, http://www.statisticbrain.com/human-brain-statistics/.

4 Medina, *Brain Rules*.

5 Rodolfo Llinás, *I of the Vortex: From Neurons to Self* (Cambridge, MA: MIT Press, 2002), 175.

- Four lobes—frontal, parietal, occipital, temporal
- Three pounds and three main parts—cerebrum, cerebellum, and brain stem
- Two hemispheres (right and left) and two speech centers (Broca's and Wernicke's)
- One hundred billion neurons—one whole brain

Your brain is the consummate mover and shaker of your existence. It thinks, it anticipates, and it has all sorts of moving parts. It reacts consciously and subconsciously. It emotes and changes. In short, it amazes. Humans are the only heel-to-toe walking creature on earth and have the largest brain per body size in the animal kingdom. It only makes sense that we understand how to cater to its needs.

Our brain is the ultimate multitasker.

We are born with an average of nearly 100 billion neurons, and, luckily for us, those are the learner cells. In a feat nothing less than miraculous, the brain prunes away extra neurons (from 200 billion in utero—yes, the fetus has twice as many neurons as we adults do, even though a newborn's brain weighs a mere 12 ounces[6]) to maximize connections we use. In order for information to be useful, neurons need to connect. Those connections equate to learning.

From a biological standpoint, all learning is about change. Judy Willis, neuroscientist-turned-educator, captures her middle schoolers' imaginations by equating learning to "bloodless brain surgery," while others support the notion of teachers as brain changers. James Zull realizes that "if a teacher has any success at all, she has produced physical change in her student's brain. Teaching is the art of changing the brain."[7] What they are talking about is the act of creating conditions that lead to change in a learner's brain, not controlling it or otherwise rearranging it.

Learning, in its basic form, tends to consist of four steps:

1. The brain receives some sort of input.
2. The brain reflects, analyzes, and makes necessary connections.
3. The brain cobbles the bits and pieces together, manipulating the information to make meaning.
4. The brain exhorts us to do something with it, apply it, or take some sort of action and test it out.[8]

At a basic neurological level, those steps look like this:

- If a child takes in information through her sensory pathways and her brain makes the decision to keep that knowledge, the integra-

6 "Human Brain Statistics."

7 James Zull, *The Art of Changing the Brain* (Sterling, VA: Stylus, 2002).

8 David Kolb, *Experiential Learning: Experience as the Source of Learning and Development* (Upper Saddle River, NJ: Prentice Hall, 2014).

tive process takes over and makes sense out of that learning as she sleeps.

- This consolidation occurs when neurons transmit messages to one another. The messages must cross microscopic gaps between the neurons—laboriously at first, and then more quickly with each subsequent moment of access.
- Eventually the learning is connected to several points within a denser and denser web of neurons, easing the information retrieval process for the conscious learner, which, in turn, makes it more likely the learner can apply her knowledge.[9]

These elements are not always linear or sequential, and as you know, we can vacillate between reflection and manipulating ideas over and over. We may test things and return to generating more ideas. What this learning cycle does is remind us that it is not enough for our learners to have information—they must use the idea and action parts of the brain and apply what they know. And we as teachers know this: when this happens, learning is cemented more readily into long-term memory.

Scholars like Tony Wagner and Daniel Willingham say the innovators of the future will be students who can formulate the "right questions," sift through overwhelming amounts of information, and clearly communicate knowledge they have recombined in original ways.[10] What can neuroscience show us about developing students'

critical thinking skills? About changing the way we approach teaching and learning?

As I mentioned, learning develops an ever-expanding network of neural connections within the brain. When students practice higher-order thinking—when they question an initial assumption or answer and explore it further—more connections and pathways are created in the brain. Challenge fuels this growth. This also occurs when students are able to recombine their new knowledge with what they've learned in the past.[11] Edu-sketching and its inherently synesthetic thought is perfect for such exploration and recombination. Using the visual, auditory, and kinesthetic modes, along with a combination of past and current knowledge, aligns precisely with what we as educators want our students to do. Let's look at the brain itself and how this expansion of neural networks is accomplished.

THE BIOLOGY OF LEARNING

Three major physical components of the brain are the brain stem, the cerebellum, and the cerebral hemispheres of the cerebrum. The brain stem is located at the top of the spinal cord, at the base of the brain, and is the ultimate multitasker, connecting higher areas

---

9 Wendi Pillars, "Teachers as Brain-Changers: Neuroscience and Learning," *Education Week*, December 20, 2011, http://www.edweek.org/tm/articles/2011/12/20/tln_pillars.html.

10 T. Wagner, *The Global Achievement Gap: Why Even the Best Schools Don't*

Teach the New Skills Our Students Need—and What We Can Do About It (New York: Basic Books, 2010); D. Willingham, *Why Students Don't Like School: A Cognitive Scientist Answers Questions About How the Mind Works and What It Means for the Classroom* (San Francisco: Jossey-Bass, 2010).

11 Pillars, "Teachers as Brain-Changers."

of the brain to the spinal cord and keeping them alert. It is also responsible for maintaining basic physiological and automatic functions such as swallowing, facial sensations, breathing, and sleeping. The cerebellum is located adjacent to the brain stem and is the master coordinator for timing and movement, monitoring impulses from nerve endings in the muscles. Known as the "little brain," it is crucially involved in learning, performing, and timing complex motor tasks, including speaking. Scientists have recently claimed that along with the motor function automaticity, the cerebellum also stores learning that is rote and repetitive (think multiplication facts, particular dates, or how to tie a shoelace).[12]

The two cerebral hemispheres comprise the bulk of the brain weight, and each hemisphere is controlled by nerves in the opposite hemisphere. The corpus callosum contains over 250 million nerve fibers. It connects the right and left hemispheres, while serving as the communication and coordination bridge between them during that information crossover. Keep in mind that original processing of information can happen in nanoseconds, but longer-term storage may take days or even months.

As you learn more about how the whole brain learns and creates connections, you will realize how unlikely it is that our right and left hemispheres are singular units acting independently of each other, or with clearly delineated tasks. Despite the theories of people being right-brained or left-brained, it's important to note that there is continual interplay between the brain's two hemispheres. More logical thinking is still attributed to the left hemisphere, though, as more holistic and creative aspects of cognition are to the right. And while the left hemisphere controls the right side of the body, and the right hemisphere controls the left side of the body, it takes both hemispheres to support our thinking. Edu-sketching marries the hemispheres nicely, born of auditory, visual, and kinesthetic strengths, while zipping information back and forth between the lobes in a process of synthesis.

Covering the cerebral hemispheres is a thin layer called the cerebral cortex (cortex is Latin for "tree bark"). The very newest and most recently evolved part of the brain is known as the neocortex, in charge of rationality and logic. (Unfortunately the limbic system is more dominant, which is why we let emotion get the better of us sometimes.) The cerebral cortex is the location of six layers of nerve cells stunningly enmeshed in approximately 10,000 miles of connecting fibers per cubic inch.[13] The cortex envelops the brain and has three primary functions: sensing input from the outside world, integrating all the sensory bits and pieces, and acting upon that knowledge in some way. Its physical delicacy belies its resilience to withstand and control such monumental rigors. This covering has evolved to be about the size of an open newspaper, and all those squiggly lines (sulci and gyri, to be exact) come from scrunching it up to fit inside the space of your cranium. (Most other mammals have a smooth cortex.) This neocortex, or outer layer, of the brain is where our higher-level thinking happens, and is also the site of many

---

12 M. Sprenger, *Wiring the Brain for Reading: Brain-Based Strategies* (San Francisco: Jossey-Bass, 2013).

13 D. Sousa, *How the Special Needs Brain Learns* (Thousand Oaks, CA: Corwin Press, 2001).

scanned brain activities—hence our knowledge of various motor and sensory areas, as well as visual, auditory, and olfactory.

Despite the rapid growth of the neocortex in our early childhood years, no new nerve cells actually form here. Instead, the massive growth comes from dendrites networking and extending exponentially as they receive input from other nerve cells.[14] (Dendrites receive, while axons send out, information.) The more use they get, the more they grow in number, and although growth occurs well into old age, the greatest growth occurs from ages 0–10. If the connections are not used or retrieved frequently enough, or are damaged in some way, the neurons decrease and die off. This cell death is known as apoptosis. Although estimates of cell death per day hover around 18 million, it's not necessarily a bad thing. With 100 billion neurons, it would take a few hundred years to completely void our neuronal stash, to lose our marbles completely, as it were.

The cortex is split down the middle into a right and left hemisphere and can be further divided into the back and front cortex. In a very general sense, the back part (sensory and integrative cortex) receives and remembers, while the front (motor and frontal integrative cortex) generates ideas and actions.[15] It constitutes a whopping 70% of the nervous system.[16]

The back integrative cortex receives sensory input, and is also

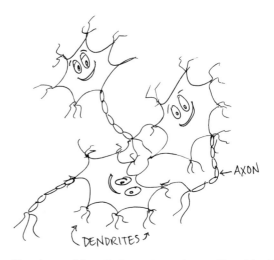

Growth and learning result from the interaction and networking of dendrites and axons. Dendrites receive information while axons send it out. It's a miraculous system.

home to long-term memory, the past, and points of connection. Memories, emotions linked to those memories and experiences, facts and names, and so on, are all functions associated with this area. The front integrative cortex differs because it's about predicting, creating, taking the abstract, and making choices or creating associations in the future. Responsibility and decision making call this area home. Think of reaching "back" physically for past experiences and "forward" for predicting—our brains really know so much more than we give them credit for—and you have a ready-made visual for your students.

---

14 M. Diamond, "The Brain . . . Use It or Lose It," Johns Hopkins School of Education, 2012, http://education.jhu.edu/PD/newhorizons/Neurosciences/articles/The%20Brain...Use%20it%20or%20Lose%20It/.

15 James Zull, *The Art of Changing the Brain* (Sterling, VA: Stylus, 2002), 35.

16 E. Jensen, *Brain-Based Learning* (Thousand Oaks, CA: Corwin Press, 2008).

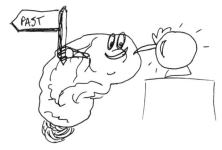

Your brain is a master at the simultaneous acts of looking forward and looking back.

Within the cerebrum are four primary lobes: the frontal, temporal, occipital, and parietal lobes, each named for their corresponding skull bones. The occipital lobes are at the back of the brain, and are home to the visual cortex—which, in conjunction with all things visual, is a critical area for reading. As a matter of fact, there is even what's known as a "letterbox" region in the left occipitotemporal area.[17] This area typically lights up in response when it sees written words, but when people are asked orally to think of specific aspects of letters (whether strokes are above or below the line, for example) or how words are spelled, it will also light up. Scientists have thus determined this area of the brain to be one of visual analysis.

This activation of the letterbox region is consistent in brains scanned, but what is even more fascinating to me is the finding that parts of this area consistently process specific visual stimuli. Houses and landscapes activate the area of this lobe nearest the midline, but as you move toward the side of the brain, there are regions that prefer faces, then the written word, and at the brain's edge, objects and tools. Scientists have even found that the hemispheres sort words into the left hemisphere, while faces are processed in the right. Mag-netoencephalography has even shown how words presented on the left side of the visual field are processed in the right hemisphere, and words presented on the right are processed in the left hemisphere. Even though scientists have narrowed down these areas of preference, it's important to note that what they have viewed in brain scans are the peak impulses, not necessarily the underlying processes.

Parietal lobes help integrate all sorts of sensory information, including tactile, auditory, and visual information entering the brain. They, too, are important areas for reading. Temporal lobes are above our ears and are primarily responsible for hearing, speech, and some memory. The frontal lobes are right behind our forehead. They take up nearly half of the volume of the cerebrum with their functions of reasoning, higher-level thinking, expressive language, emotional restraint, personality, planning, problem solving, and curiosity—just a few of the frontal lobes' so-called executive functions. This is where decision making happens (or not), based on stored memories and emotions forwarded from the amygdala, home of instinctive fight-or-flight emotions.

As for the hemispheres, there has been much talk about left-brained versus right-brained individuals, but as you can tell by the many overlapping jobs of each area of the brain, any attempt to view the brain in motion as separate entities greatly oversimplifies its endless activities. It must be remembered that execution of even the most mundane of simple tasks requires the coordination and collaboration of a vast array of faculties. Blood flow and electrical activity have been observed in one, both, and across hemispheres, with a thicker corpus callosum resulting from communication of the hemispheres. (Studies have actually found correlations between callosal

17 S. Dehaene, *Reading in the Brain* (New York: Penguin, 2009).

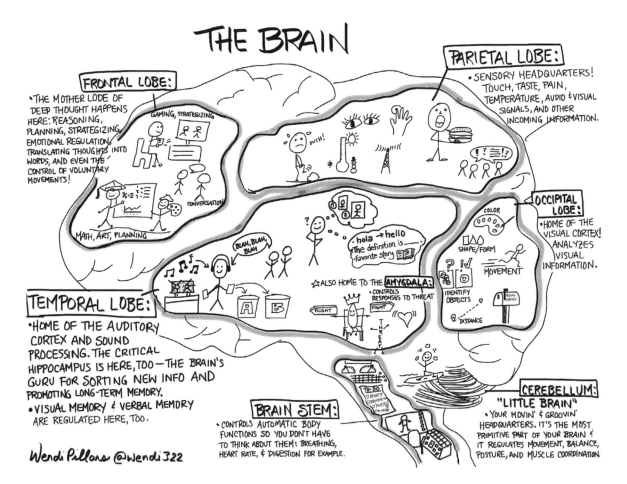

thickening and higher intelligence measures, affirming the efficiency and intellectual value of interhemispheric chatter.[18])

Imagine saying "good-bye" to a friend: words and word meanings are processed in the left hemisphere, but tone and prosody (pitch, tone, and rhythm) of speech and the emotional components of language are processed in the right. The activity behind such a "simple task" is awe inspiring, and assures us that it is not so simple after all. Or imagine reading about a sensitive topic such as slavery, as the words are primarily processed in the left hemisphere, and the right lends emotion, empathy, and more lasting resonance. Having students bring these mental images and emotions to light, to see them more clearly and consciously engage with them longer, is key to deeper learning.

WHY IS THIS KNOWLEDGE IMPORTANT TO US AS EDUCATORS?

Knowing this information lends a biological basis to what we do while encouraging increased respect for all that does go right in our thinking processes. If we only deliver information—thereby feeding

---

18 E. Luders, K. L. Narr, R. M. Bilder, P. M. Thompson, P. R. Szeszko, L. Hamilton, and A. W. Toga, "Positive Correlations Between Corpus Callosum Thickness and Intelligence," *Neuroimage* 37, no. 4 (2007): 1457–1464, doi: 10.1016/j.neuroimage.2007.06.028; Weiwei Men, Dean Falk, Tao Sun, Weibo Chen, Jianqi Li, Dazhi Yin, Lili Zang, and Mingxia Fan, "The Corpus Callosum of Albert Einstein's Brain: Another Clue to His High Intelligence?," *Brain* 137, pt. 4 (2014):e268. doi: 10.1093/brain/awt252.

the back cortex—we neglect the appetite of the frontal cortex for experimentation and testing ideas. This is the biological reason for our best practices. If we understand that so many different areas of the brain play a role in reading and comprehending what we read, then we know the reason behind multisensory and multimodal learning activities. If we understand why neurons need repetition and an emotional hook, we value making the time to do so. We can then take it a step further: if we know that the same areas are activated for visual work and reading, then we know it makes sense to strengthen both. Likewise, if we understand that learners are not completely "left-brained" or "right-brained," we can ensure we include activities that combine each hemisphere's penchant for logical versus more holistic thinking. Combining this information with opportunities to reflect, integrate, then test and act upon our thinking is the alchemy our learners need, and also need to do. They need opportunities to change their brains, and to do so means opportunities to transform input into output—to receive and use knowledge, which is what edu-sketching so naturally promotes. And to think that some people believe we use only 10% of our brain.

The limbic cortex, found within the cerebral cortex, is the heart of our emotions. Again, if we grasp the basics about how brain structures work—now via emotion—we can leverage that understanding to address learning from different angles for our students' needs. The amygdala is one part of this limbic cortex, located in the back cortex area; remember this back area is where the brain makes meaning of something—which is also precisely what the amygdala does but in a different way. It is responsible for continual fight-or-flight monitoring; it's our internal big brother, always and subconsciously watching what's happening. Sensory signals hit this stop first, often before we are consciously aware; when the amygdala senses danger or fear, it activates basic reactions needed to survive. To do so, to react instinctively, however, learning is placed on the back burner—all that blood your body needs to react to danger is diverted from your cortex. As a result, learning won't happen when learners are in defensive mode. Engaging students in a safe space lessens the reactive nature of the amygdala, and releases energy for cognitive tasks. Here we see the neurological reason behind classroom community and creating safe spaces to learn.

As we talk about student comfort and feelings of safety, it's beneficial to remember our brain's penchant for visualizing, and how natural it can be as a default strategy. A large chunk of primate brains is devoted to vision, about 30 or so areas within the occipital, temporal, and parietal lobes, and each of these areas contains either a complete or partial map of the visual world.[19] Powerful and unending intracranial collaboration helps us see. If students are stressed, it makes sense to revert to what comes more naturally—their visual strength. I've seen students who are stressed or nervous respond almost meditatively when asked to generate visuals during a reading or response, as if the diversion was precisely what they needed to come back into an academic focus zone. Conversely, I'm sure we've all seen students seize up when required to read a text at their level, let alone one more challenging; thinking through the complexity using visuals is one way of alleviating that stress.

This sketch was created by a student plagued by reading struggles, yet he cherished—and excelled at—opportunities to express himself visually.

What fascinates me is the feedback loop that exists for vision processing. I had always believed that vision was a step-by-step process: you see something, then it gets flipped upside down in the retina, crosses hemispheres, and is then processed. Well, it turns out that there are actually more fibers going back from each stage of processing to an earlier stage than going forward to the next area.[20]

---

19 V. S. Ramachandran, *The Tell-Tale Brain* (New York: Norton, 2011), location 1135.

---

20 Ibid.

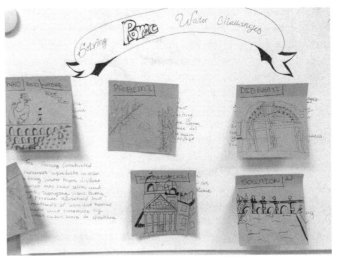

These sketches were done as part of a response during a Document-Based Question Unit on water systems used in ancient civilizations. (high school juniors and language learners)

This means our brains are constantly checking in with themselves regarding what they are seeing, comparing features and analyzing images with increasing detail. Rather than a linear process, there is a continual feedback loop. As you begin edu-sketching and imagining how to represent certain ideas, you will find yourself becoming more attentive to details. In turn, this attentiveness will demonstrate your mental feedback loop as you compare what you know to your representations on paper, then back again as you add more details.

Other parts of this loop include the hypothalamus and thalamus. The hypothalamus is the processing center for other regions of the brain and body, receiving, integrating, coordinating, and otherwise responding to information that comes its way. The thalamus connects sensory components and the higher functions of the brain. Any incoming sensory information (except smell) passes through the thalamus before being sent to the cortex.

The hippocampus, the seahorse-shaped area centralized in our brain, is a key player in both the memory process and feedback loop because here is where memories become sticky and are encoded. It holds memories of the immediate past, then compares them with experiences stored in long-term memory, which helps create meaning.[21] It also works in concert with the amygdala, recalling the emotions associated with particular memories. It is essential for encoding declarative long-term memories, which are gradually transferred to the occipital and temporal cortices.[22] One of its superpowers is that this is one area of the brain capable of generating new cells,[23] a wondrous phenomenon, especially considering this is the same area of the brain that helps create our new memories.[24] New nerve cells form in the hippocampus throughout our lives, and the more new cells, the better the encoding into long-term memory.[25]

21 M. Hardiman, *Connecting Brain Research With Effective Teaching* (Lanham, MD: Rowman and Littlefield, 2003).

22 T. Klingberg, *The Learning Brain: Memory and Brain Development in Children* (New York: Oxford University Press, 2012).

23 N. Doidge, *The Brain That Changes Itself* (New York: Viking Penguin, 2007).

24 M. Sprenger, *Wiring the Brain for Reading: Brain-Based Strategies* (San Francisco: Jossey-Bass, 2013).

25 Klingberg, *The Learning Brain*.

BRAIN CELLS

"There are billions of neurons in our brains, but what are neurons? Just cells. The brain has no knowledge until connections are made between neurons. All that we know, all that we are, comes from the way our neurons are connected."[26]

There are many brain cell varieties, but the most common are neurons and glial cells. As mentioned previously, the average brain contains around 100 billion neurons, powered by electrochemical charges. Neurons are the brain's building blocks, and their task is to create communication networks within the brain and central nervous system. The rest of the brain cells—about 90% of them—are called glial (Greek for glue) cells, which hold the neurons together and filter harmful substances out of the neurons.[27]

Glial cells are of various types, with some protecting the neurons from undesirable chemical compounds (drugs), while others help heal. Other glial cells help form the myelin sheath, a fatty sheath wrapped around the neurons that acts as insulation for the electrical impulses. Glial cells outnumber neurons ten to one, but are equally functional, and make those neurons exponentially more active,[28] contrary to initial findings that considered them mere supporting actors to neurons.

26 Tim Berners-Lee, *Weaving the Web: The Original Design and Ultimate Destiny of the World Wide Web* (New York: HarperBusiness, 1999).

27 D. Purves, G. J. Augustine, D. Fitzpatrick, et al., eds. *Neuroscience*, 2nd ed. (Sunderland, MA: Sinauer Associates , 2001).

28 N. J. Allen, and B. A. Barres. Signaling between glia and neurons: focus on synaptic plasticity. *Current Opinion in Neurobiology* 15 (2005): 542–548.

Neurons are generated throughout the embryonic stage, when the brain adds as many as 250,000 neurons a minute in the womb, with continued proliferation during the first postnatal year; by the end of the second postnatal year, the brain has reached 80% of its adult weight. Larger motor neurons, such as those that incite you to yank your hand off the hot stove, are produced first, with sensory neurons (those which respond to the internal and external environments) forming later (see Appendix B for more information on cellular phases during development).

Not all neurons produced are needed; overall, the numbers exceed the body's actual requirements, so a phase of cell death, or apoptosis, follows the proliferation phase. Apoptosis is a natural process of cell death that eliminates old or damaged neurons; when neurons die, the glial cells invade the damaged areas and engulf any dead neuronal tissue. Apoptosis ensures the growing brain isn't overloaded by cells and, in so doing, strengthens the connections formed at an incredible rate during infancy. These connections reach maximum density by age six;[29] after this stage, unused connections phase themselves out—this is the reason behind the need to maintain a stimulated brain for maximum development.

Neurons have three major anatomical parts: the cell body (soma), dendrites, and the axon (long information highway). The cell nucleus contains DNA, energy-generating mitochondria, and other machinery to help us remember—or not. Dendrites grow as neurons receive input, so the more information learned, the more dendrites grow. The basic unadorned process goes like this: dendrites (imagine the roots of a tree) reach out to receive electrical impulses from other neurons. The cell body then integrates the impulse information, and this information is subsequently transmitted to the terminals down the long axon fiber—in nanoseconds. Thanks to the thousands of dendrites and their connections, neurons can connect with upwards of 10,000 other cells, with neural connections estimated in the 100 trillions, and even quadrillions in our earliest years. Wow.

To put it in perspective, scientists say it's "at least 1,000 times the number of stars in our galaxy."[30] Even more incredible is that adults have about half the number of neurons toddlers have. Imagine how much learning is happening in curious newborns and toddlers in the first few years of life—it's no wonder when you consider that 700–1,000 new neural connections form every second.[31] That's rapid proliferation for sure, but after a few years, pruning slows it down and ensures maximal neural efficiency for all those resultant connections.

The third primary part is the axon. Despite the thousands of dendrites extending from a neuron, each has only one long, wirelike axon (although its length varies), and its primary job is to send out information to other cells. As the axons transmit information out of the cell, the myelin sheath wrapped around each axon thickens with use. The greater the myelin insulation, the faster the impulse travels. When this happens and the message transmission speeds up, far more efficient recall of information occurs in our brains. Impulses

---

29 R. Carter, *Mapping the Mind* (London: Weidenfeld and Nicolson, 1998).

30 V. Ross, "Numbers: The Nervous System, From 268-MPH Signals to Trillions of Synapses," *Discover*, March 2011, http://discovermagazine.com/2011/mar/10-numbers-the-nervous-system.

31 "Key Concepts: Brain Architecture," Harvard Center on the Developing Child, accessed September 2014, http://developingchild.harvard.edu/key_concepts/brain_architecture/.

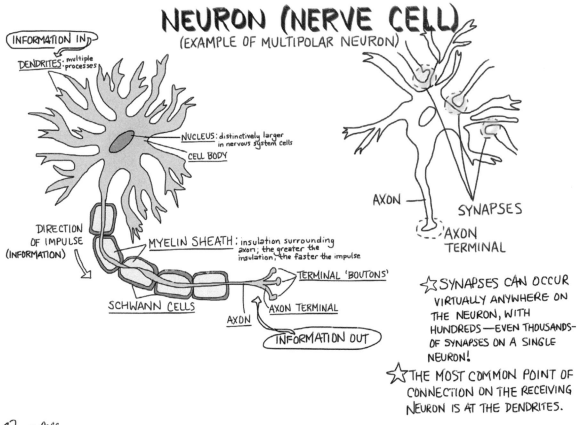

NEURON (NERVE CELL)
(EXAMPLE OF MULTIPOLAR NEURON)

INFORMATION IN

DENDRITES: multiple processes

NUCLEUS: distinctively larger in nervous system cells

CELL BODY

DIRECTION OF IMPULSE (INFORMATION)

MYELIN SHEATH: insulation surrounding axon; the greater the insulation, the faster the impulse

SCHWANN CELLS

AXON

TERMINAL 'BOUTONS'

AXON TERMINAL

INFORMATION OUT

AXON

SYNAPSES

AXON TERMINAL

☆ SYNAPSES CAN OCCUR VIRTUALLY ANYWHERE ON THE NEURON, WITH HUNDREDS—EVEN THOUSANDS—OF SYNAPSES ON A SINGLE NEURON!

☆ THE MOST COMMON POINT OF CONNECTION ON THE RECEIVING NEURON IS AT THE DENDRITES.

Wendi Pillars @wendi322

travel along the axon electrically, but then use a chemical burst to cross from one neuron to the next. Anywhere from 250 to 2,500 impulses can be transmitted by the neurons per second,[32] along the axon to the synaptic terminals. Akin to a new pathway, the more use this axon superhighway gets, the more smoothly and efficiently it can be traveled, and the more rapidly areas of the brain interconnect.

You can see how the nerve cell structure is designed specifically for creating chains of communication within the brain and throughout the body. Axons and dendrites are two of the fundamental elements for transmitting communicative impulses. This transmission is distinctive to neurons, even more so with the presence of an outer membrane to convey nerve signals as electrochemical pulses. I will now examine this transmission more closely to understand how the nerve cell uses electricity and chemicals to fuel nerve signal transmission within and along the neuron, and across the synaptic gaps.

ELECTRICAL BASICS

We hear talk of connections all the time, but what does that mean? One of the most fundamental concepts for promoting learning in the brain is the emphasis on prior knowledge, background knowledge, and activating what learners already know. Connecting, providing a hook for new or difficult concepts, and eliciting that prior

knowledge from our learners—all of this parallels the processes that occur already at the neuronal level. Understanding how nature links information and memories together lends insight into how we can become effective at providing more than just a sensory experience for our learners. Teaching and learning go hand in hand, connections at the crux of it all. But how does this happen at the neuronal level?

At the ends of the axons are axon terminals that communicate with the thousands of dendrites—but they don't even touch the dendrites, so how can they transmit information to other cells? In between the axons and dendrites of each neuron is a synaptic cleft, or gap, where molecules known as neurotransmitters act as couriers to transport information across the cleft. This is where the chemical burst mentioned above comes in.

The 50-plus known neurotransmitters are composed of protein molecules. Smaller-molecule neurotransmitters are amino acids, while larger ones consist of peptides—proteins made up of several smaller amino acids, hence their moniker neuropeptides. They are created in the cell body and stored in the vesicles at the terminal boutons, which prepare the information to be transmitted across the synapse to an awaiting dendrite of the next neuron. Generally there are vesicles containing and releasing one neurotransmitter and one neuropeptide. Some of these neurotransmitters are thought to be valuable in cognitive processes; following are just a couple, but they demonstrate the various roles assumed by the neurotransmitters.

Perhaps you've heard of dopamine, or a dopamine surge that comes from predicting outcomes or solving a puzzle. Dopamine is an example of a neurotransmitter believed to be involved in working

---

32 J. Beatty, *The Human Brain: Essentials of Behavioral Neuroscience* (Thousand Oaks, CA: Sage, 2001).

memory, motivation, and addiction due to feelings of reward and pleasure when it is released. It is linked to pleasure seeking and risk taking. Creating circumstances within our classroom where students feel safe to try new things and attempt challenges without fear of ridicule, and challenging students without overwhelming them will help them attain the "aha moment" more readily. Because dopamine is a key player in movement, we can also increase its production with some gross motor movements, like 5-minute energizers that get our students up out of their seats or quick games.

Noradrenaline (or norepinephrine) is more concentrated within the brain, and its levels increase dramatically when we awaken. Its release is central in maintaining and focusing attention, and ensures that weak neural connections are pruned away while stronger ones flourish. Since it affects the amygdala, it undergirds fight-or-flight responses. This is the neurotransmitter that increases heart rate and blood flow, hence the brain's oxygen supply. Think adrenaline. Risk taking, anything exciting (which we know varies daily with our students), friendly competition, time constraints, and, oh yeah—being in love (sigh . . . the drama has an upside), will all encourage its release.

Why does this matter? It is stunning to know that we can influence learning at the neuronal level in our students. We are physically able to change someone's brain. If that doesn't amaze us, the responsibility of what we are tasked to do on a daily basis should. As educators, we are responsible for teaching our students academic

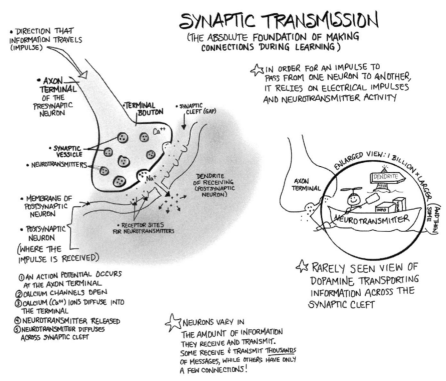

SYNAPTIC TRANSMISSION
(THE ABSOLUTE FOUNDATION OF MAKING CONNECTIONS DURING LEARNING)

★ IN ORDER FOR AN IMPULSE TO PASS FROM ONE NEURON TO ANOTHER, IT RELIES ON ELECTRICAL IMPULSES AND NEUROTRANSMITTER ACTIVITY

• DIRECTION THAT INFORMATION TRAVELS (IMPULSE)

• AXON TERMINAL OF THE PRESYNAPTIC NEURON

• TERMINAL BOUTON

• SYNAPTIC CLEFT (GAP)

Ca++

• SYNAPTIC VESSICLE
• NEUROTRANSMITTERS

Na+

• MEMBRANE OF POSTSYNAPTIC NEURON

DENDRITE OF RECEIVING (POSTSYNAPTIC NEURON)

• POSTSYNAPTIC NEURON
(WHERE THE IMPULSE IS RECEIVED)

• RECEPTOR SITES FOR NEUROTRANSMITTERS

① AN ACTION POTENTIAL OCCURS AT THE AXON TERMINAL
② CALCIUM CHANNELS OPEN
③ CALCIUM (Ca++) IONS DIFFUSE INTO THE TERMINAL
④ NEUROTRANSMITTER RELEASED
⑤ NEUROTRANSMITTER DIFFUSES ACROSS SYNAPTIC CLEFT

ENLARGED VIEW: 1 BILLION x LARGER (AND THEN)

AXON TERMINAL

DENDRITE

INFO

NEUROTRANSMITTER

★ RARELY SEEN VIEW OF DOPAMINE, TRANSPORTING INFORMATION ACROSS THE SYNAPTIC CLEFT

★ NEURONS VARY IN THE AMOUNT OF INFORMATION THEY RECEIVE AND TRANSMIT. SOME RECEIVE & TRANSMIT THOUSANDS OF MESSAGES, WHILE OTHERS HAVE ONLY A FEW CONNECTIONS!

content, and social and emotional skills, and doing so in the most informed manner. For me, understanding these processes at the neuronal level has deepened my attention to students' individual learning, and has helped me discern between practices that are truly brain based and those that are not.

So, you've learned a bit about neurotransmitters, and you know they are used to communicate with other neurons in the brain. But how does that happen? Basically, neurons release the neurotransmitters once an action potential is generated. The neurotransmitter will send one of two messages: (1) excitatory, letting the information pass from the cell body along the axon; or (2) inhibitory, preventing passage along the axon. I hope this isn't too complicated, but if you look at the drawings, they will help you understand the important tasks of the neurons. Once you are able to break it down, well, then this is some pretty cool information to pass along to your students.

Here we go. Technically speaking, the neuron letting go of information is the presynaptic neuron, while the one across the cleft—the receiver—becomes the postsynaptic neuron. This release occurs after an electrical stimulation; the neuron can choose to turn itself off (inhibition) or go with the stimulation (excitation) and allow the information to pass on to the postsynaptic neuron. This sounds far simpler than it is—but it arms you with the basics of how the brain learns. I like how John Medina describes the synaptic environment: imagine two trees being uprooted by giant hands, turned 90 degrees so the roots face each other, and then jammed together;[33] you can

visualize the real world of neurons, a.k.a. the "holy neural ground" of the learning brain. Connections galore—each represents information being stored or recalled. Learning and memory are attributed to the connected neural pathways, and how strong those connections are. This strengthening process is known as long-term potentiation.[34]

Think of the neuron as a battery, with its ability to generate voltage. This voltage is called the membrane potential in the nerve cell. Every cell in the body contains electricity, and each atom has free-floating particles called ions. Ions have either a negative or positive charge, and equilibrium of their voltage charge is maintained because they are diffused both inside and outside of the neuron. Neurons keep extra positive ions outside their cell membrane, and extra negative ions inside. The ion separation results from the selectivity of tiny channels in the neuronal membrane, channels that permit only certain ions in and out. Some remain open continuously and others open only momentarily; this means the neuron is semipermeable. Neurons also have a pump mechanism to move ions in and out of the cell to maintain or restore their equilibrium. How fast an ion moves through the channels depends on the impetus from the electrochemical charge, whether the appropriate channel is open, and whether the appropriate ion is present when the channel is open.

Membrane voltage, in essence, hinges on the effectiveness of the semipermeability of the membrane and the ability to maintain charge separation. As noted earlier, the inside of the neuron is differ-

---

33 Medina, *Brain Rules*, 56.

34 "Long-Term Potentiation," Wikipedia, accessed September 2014, http://en.wikipedia.org/wiki/Long-term_potentiation.

ent from the fluid outside the cell; this potential difference is known as the resting membrane potential or simply resting potential. Different neurons have slightly different resting potentials. ("Potential" refers to the source of electrical activity.)

Nerve cells are unique in their ability to manipulate the flow of charged ions across the cell membrane. Since nerve cells deal in information, the changes in charges are what constitute information for the neurons. If the voltage becomes more positive, it is depolarized; if it's more negative, it is hyperpolarized.[35] Another particular voltage is known as the threshold,[36] which occurs after positive ions from fluid outside the neuron enter the neuron through channels opened for the tiniest fraction of a second. A chain reaction of positive charges occurs, which in turn generates an action potential.[37]

ACTION POTENTIAL

Once an action potential has started, or fired, it is "difficult to stop," according to brain scientist Rodolfo Llinas.[38] The action potential travels like a wave from a point on the axon to the presynaptic terminals, where they prepare to contact other neurons at synaptic gaps. As seen above, a typical nerve signal involves a change in electrical

strength, and the average nerve signal takes about 203 milliseconds to travel past any point on the cell membrane. Signals originate from sensory organs (eyes, ears) and inner sensors (those which monitor blood pressure, temperature, etc.) with billions of signals sent and received every second.

We can see how the maxim "use it or lose it" applies to neurons: connections that are used more grow stronger and become more permanent. Those used less fade away through a normal process called pruning. And with literally thousands of dendrites at the end of each axon, the brain is an extraordinarily efficient learning machine.

WHY IS THIS SO IMPORTANT TO KNOW?

Neurons connecting is precisely what creates our learning. Without connections forming, changing, and speeding up or slowing down, we wouldn't be able to change our brains, in either the physical or mental sense. If the action potential doesn't occur, neither does learning.

Those 100 billion neurons we are born with? They exist, but their quadrillion connections do not—at least not right away, though 700–1,000 new synapses per second are forming, especially in the first 5 years of a child's life.[39] And they keep on forming. As educators, our top job is to foster connections, not only between our students and

---

35 For those of you who really must know, more positive means closer to 0 mV, while more negative means more negative than –70 mV.

36 If you must know, –55 mV. Llinás, *I of the Vortex*.

37 S. Greenfield, *Brain Story: Unlocking Our Inner World of Emotions, Memories, Ideas, and Desires* (London: BBC Worldwide, 2000).

38 Llinás, *I of the Vortex*, 86.

39 Pia Britto, "How Childrens' Brains Develop—New Insights," Unicef Connect, May 14, 2014, http://blogs.unicef.org/2014/05/14/how-childrens-brains

us, but among the many hungry neurons in our students' brains. Because this is a monumental task, it only makes sense to relay this information to the students so they, too, realize that their brains are in a constant state of change. The brains they leave home with in the morning are not the ones they fall asleep with at night. I don't know about you, but wow, is that fascinating! The greater their under-standing about what's happening inside their brains, the more deeply students trust our strategies, our reasons for repetition and review, spiraled information, questioning about prior knowledge, and making connections, among others. Hence, the more they can take charge of their own learning.

I hope as you've read through this chapter you have been synthe-sizing ideas in a way you can present to your students. We've delved from the outer part of our amazing brain, the neocortex and its dif-ferent functions, down through the two hemispheres, into the four lobes, and even further into the center, where the hippocampus lies, replete with access to our memories and power to form new ones. From there we dove deep into the cellular level to learn about neu-rons and how interconnections among them are so crucial to learn-ing and memory. And along the way, we came to understand the internal significance of the phrase "making connections" in the realm of true education—in addition to the external connections we nurture with our students.

How might you create a visual for the process of learning? A neu-ron with all of its parts? Connections between neurons? The trans-mission of information? Can you create a flowchart to explain learning and how information crosses a synapse?

What other pieces of information do you think your students would want to know? Can you envision places in your instruction and planning where you can reiterate this information?

As for spiraling and accessing prior knowledge, how did you fare on your anticipation guide from the beginning of the chapter? How many of the questions can you answer with certainty after reading this chapter? If you learned even one new answer, guess what hap-pened inside your brain? More importantly, how would you visualize that?

And what do these things all have in common?

-develop-new-insights/. By the way, this link contains some wonderful visual notes by Image Think.

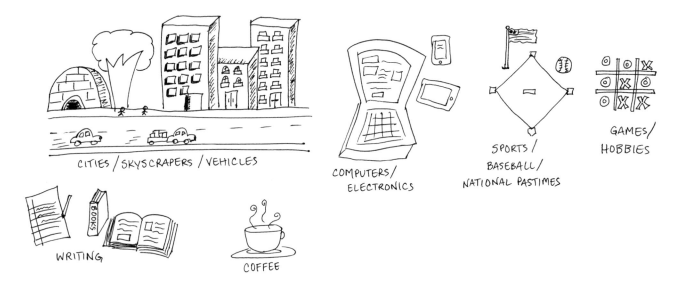

CITIES / SKYSCRAPERS / VEHICLES

COMPUTERS/
ELECTRONICS

SPORTS /
BASEBALL/
NATIONAL PASTIMES

GAMES/
HOBBIES

WRITING

COFFEE

These were all created by neurons connecting, by action potentials and neurotransmitters like dopamine and noradrenaline transmitting information along axons and across synapses. This is fascinating but, more importantly, absolutely necessary for educators to understand. This is what learning is. And when we talk about applications in the classroom, you can imagine all of the connections occurring, how the flow state encourages the release of dopamine, and how the excitement of making connections can encourage the release of noradrenaline.

If connections among our 100 billion neurons can create such wonders, you can certainly nudge your students to try their hand at sketching.

ANSWERS TO QUIZ

1. T
2. c
3. F
4. T
5. F
6. b
7. F
8. T
9. F
10. F

CHAPTER THREE

All Hail the Visual

When words don't work, thinking doesn't work. . . . Words have become our default thinking tool.
> —*Dan Roam,* Blah, Blah, Blah: What to Do
> When Words Don't Work

The world needs all kinds of minds, and some of those minds think in pictures.
> —*Temple Grandin, author and speaker*

I SEE WHAT YOU MEAN

So there's this little guy in your brain. With the moniker of Homunculus, he's unforgettable, if not a bit grotesquely disproportionate. This little man represents a sensory map of the human body, with each part sized according to how much sensory information is processed there. Facial features are expansive, ranking right up there behind hands and feet, according to your brain. And yes, genitalia. The larger the homunculus features, the greater their sensory perception. It's a fascinating and provocative visual, for sure, and one that, at a glance, demonstrates the rapidity with which we process visuals. It demonstrates the ease with which a visual can sometimes capture what would otherwise take oodles of text to describe or explain. That visual will stick with you much longer than a page full of text could ever dream of.

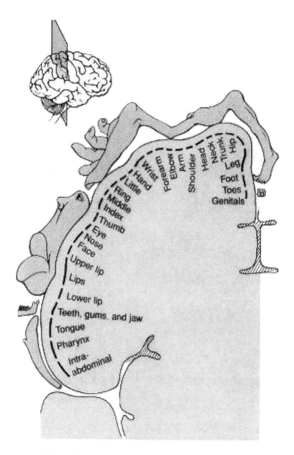

(a) Somatosensory cortex in right cerebral hemisphere

Images can be far more memorable than mere words—some are extremely vivid. *Source*: OpenStax College, Anatomy & Physiology, Connexions Web site. http://cnx.org/content/col11496/1.6/, June 19, 2013.

We owe a lot more credit to the visual side of things for all ages of learners. In Chapter 2 we learned about just how powerful vision and visualizing are for our memory and learning. Reading is visual. By default, so is the bulk of our learning. Why wouldn't we want to enhance our students' visual language capabilities? What holds us back from using them more?

Visualization and attentive observation are critical components for the encoding and retrieval of memories. Edu-sketching synthesizes information from multiple sources and taps into creativity, the arts, and even metaphorical thinking. Its uses are many in the assessment realm too, both formative and summative; it makes sense for us as educators to pay heed to imagery.

As educators, we want our students to

- learn new information;
- remember new information;
- be able to connect information to something else they've learned—because we know it makes the most sense that way;
- and then be able to apply and/or transfer that knowledge in other scenarios.

One of the ways to do this is to delve into the brain's natural tendencies and powers within the learning processes (Chapter 2). Recall that any experience modifies the brain by strengthening or weakening the synapses linking neurons together. This type of modification is what we so blithely call learning, as if it weren't something utterly impressive. Recall, too, that there are multiple feedback loops during each processing stage—it's not linear. And to up the ante, all of this wiring is incredibly malleable all the way through adulthood—

we humans have been endowed with lifelong neuroplasticity. And guess what that means? Even if you say you can't draw, your brain says you can. Um ... guess who's smarter (and ready to be challenged).

Then, remember where vision occurs. (Hint: it's not in the eye.)[1] Yes, that large chunk of your occipital, temporal, and parietal lobes is deeply devoted to vision, all 30-plus visual areas housed in your brain. No one seems to know just why we have so many visual areas, but they are specialized for all kinds of things: color, movement, horizontal lines, vertical lines, faces, different shapes, and so on. The visual cortex even splits into "how and what" pathways that distinguish between an overall layout of objects (not just a singular location) and an automatic catlike sense of how to navigate through that layout.[2]

Before we continue, I should note that although we all have areas in the brain devoted to visual processing, no two brains are exactly alike. The areas and pathways recruited will differ among learners, and because multiple brain regions have a role in storing information, memories are actually scattered across the brain. Your brain dissects and redistributes information instantaneously: vertical and horizontal lines, colors, and—holy moly—even vowels and consonants are stored separately.[3] Even bilingual speakers, who learn and use their two languages in different contexts, and for different reasons, store their languages in the different areas of the brain.[4]

---

1 Vision occurs in the brain. Remember from Chapter 2.

2 V. S. Ramachandran, *The Tell-Tale Brain* (New York: Norton, 2011).

3 J. Medina, *Brain Rules* (Seattle, WA: Pear Press, 2008).

4 I. King, "The Neurolinguistics of Bilingualism," English Language and Lin-

Sometimes verbal descriptions will evoke imagery so powerful and vivid, you can't help but sketch it. "The moment of encoding (learning) is . . . 'Like a blender left running with the lid left off—information is literally sliced into discrete pieces as it enters the brain and splattered all over the insides of our mind—signals from different sensory sources are registered in separate brain areas.'" (Medina, *Brain Rules*, 104)

Bottom line? How you see and store information will be different from the way I do. And the way you see and store information will be different from every single one of your students. Some need lots of repetition and intense attention, while others seem to learn as if by osmosis. Longer-lasting memories will form the more elaborately the information is presented. In other words, use multiple channels to get information in, and you're more likely to get information out when you and your students need it.

As we consider the benefits of seeing things differently in this chapter, my goal is to raise your consciousness about how you are already using many of these strategies, not only with your students, but also in your everyday thinking. Once you realize how much you already have in your visual toolbox, you will be surprised how easy it is to imagine, and plan for, ways to use some of these ideas in your classroom.

guistics, St. Olaf College, 2010, http://www.stolaf.edu/depts/ciswp/iking/engl250 .html.

When we think about seeing things differently as educators, there are three important questions to ponder:

- How do we view our instruction?
- How do our students view our instruction?
- Is our instruction more about our content or our students' learning?

Within the classroom, sometimes teachers are guilty (myself included) of being Drone Masters. On and on we go, perilously unaware of the glazed stares and disengagement. And we get frustrated when students don't remember the most minute of details. Sometimes we just hope they will read our minds, believing they "should get this" as we assign the next task without sufficient support. Either way, their ability to understand and connect knowledge is weakened, if not destroyed.

THE COMPLEXITY OF SIMPLE SKETCHES

Students are far more engaged when visuals are involved, whether with edu-sketches or other images. Face it, some of the textbooks are boring. If you're not supplementing textbooks with images, your kids are missing out on richer thinking. Encouraging visual note-taking, even for students who are able to take great verbal notes, helps them more deeply understand the content when drawing images to represent concepts. Visual note-taking extracts the passivity of even the most well-written notes because it demands active processing and recall.

Young children, toddler age, draw apparently random lines on paper but can tell you an entire story about what those lines represent. Children are hard-wired to make sense of the world they see around them; they start to scribble, then draw, randomly at first, then more identifiably. No more tadpole bodies. Pictures are a mainstay of a kid's world—why should that change as we get older? And from Chapter 2, we know why, thanks to the brain's extreme penchant for visuals.

My own son reminded me dearly (she says in hindsight) of Harold in *Harold and the Purple Crayon* the day he, in his little white footie pajamas and blond wisps of hair, drew across our white cabinets and leather couch with a purple marker.[5] Although I'm not sure how adroitly he blended his real and fantasy worlds together like Harold did, it made me want to . . . reread the book again. *Harold and the Purple Crayon* is a time-honored children's book in which a pajama-clad Harold creates his own world, complete with problems and solutions, with a single purple crayon.

Despite the simplicity of Harold's bold line drawings, the machinations of his thinking make it real, with actual causes and effects. He has to fashion his escape from dragons and draw his way out of the water, among other adventures. Conceptual blending makes this story work; we can read it, watch the "real" Harold drawing, dare I say, "fictional realities" (for us, they're fiction; for him, they're very real), and allow those ideas to exist side by side in our minds. Sometimes, the simpler the drawing, the better—drawing only needs to represent 30% of reality for us to recognize it. We can do that.

As *Harold and the Purple Crayon* shows us, the books that have the power to engage us are the ones that tap into our brain's visual and verbal areas, while allowing us to imagine a third story. A happy brain is one whose wholeness and myriad skills are being optimized. Generating ideas and brainstorming, sequencing, linking, connecting, mapping, visioning, planning, finding solutions, and clarifying are just a few of a happy brain's many favorite things to do—in both its seemingly tentacled visual and verbal areas. You see how happy Harold is in the midst of his illustrated, imagined adventures. The whole brain is at play for him and for the reader, as we wonder along with him.

What are you doing to keep your students' whole brains happy? How can you view your instruction now?

Below is a page from a planning book. You can see where visuals stop—right at third grade. We rely heavily on pictures when we are learning to read. Business leaders know how to distill salient points in graphics. Great presenters rely on images to hook, punctuate, and enhance their message. And if you feel like rebutting, saying it takes too much time to get images, think about this: if your content is important, then it's worth the time for you to present it in a way that makes it equally so for your students.

Drawing your own counts. The more we draw in class, especially as we talk, the more we boil down to the essence. The more students see us draw, the more willing they are to try it. The main idea is for the images to cue recognition—think of one or two prominent visuals to represent specific concepts. What would be a good visual to represent Manifest Destiny or the Reformation? Yes, there's time for detail, too, but if the essence is solidly understood, those details will have a hook on which to hang.

In class, combined words and pictures are both powerful and practical. Depending on your purpose, you can have more or fewer

_____

5 C. Johnson, *Harold and the Purple Crayon* (New York: Harper Collins, 1955).

Instructional Strategies for Phonics and Word Recognition

Demonstration	Grade-Level Standards																						
	K				1							2						3				4	5
	a	b	c	d	a	b	c	d	e	f	g	a	b	c	d	e	f	a	b	c	d	a	a
Environmental Print Study	✓	✓																					
First Reads	✓	✓	✓	✓																			
Mine to Learn			✓								✓												
Drawing and Labeling	✓	✓				✓	✓	✓		✓		✓	✓	✓	✓		✓	✓					
Word Building	✓	✓		✓	✓	✓	✓			✓		✓	✓				✓						
Word and Part Study	✓	✓		✓	✓	✓	✓	✓	✓	✓	✓	✓	✓	✓	✓	✓	✓	✓	✓	✓	✓	✓	✓
Retrospective Miscue Analysis: Words					✓	✓	✓	✓	✓	✓	✓	✓	✓	✓	✓	✓	✓	✓	✓	✓	✓	✓	✓
Spelling in Parts							✓	✓	✓	✓			✓	✓	✓	✓	✓	✓	✓	✓	✓	✓	✓
Tricky Passages							✓	✓	✓	✓			✓	✓	✓	✓	✓	✓	✓	✓	✓	✓	✓
Parts Analysis													✓	✓			✓	✓	✓	✓	✓	✓	✓
Morphological Analysis																		✓				✓	✓

Collaborative Engagement	Grade-Level Standards																						
	K				1							2						3				4	5
	a	b	c	d	a	b	c	d	e	f	g	a	b	c	d	e	f	a	b	c	d	a	a
Word Concentration		✓							✓														
Scrambled Words		✓			✓				✓														
Word Sorts	✓	✓		✓	✓	✓	✓	✓	✓	✓		✓	✓	✓	✓	✓		✓	✓	✓			
Partner Reading	✓	✓	✓	✓	✓	✓	✓	✓	✓	✓	✓	✓	✓	✓	✓	✓	✓	✓	✓	✓	✓	✓	✓
Partner Writing	✓	✓	✓	✓	✓	✓	✓	✓	✓	✓	✓	✓	✓	✓	✓	✓	✓	✓	✓	✓	✓	✓	✓
Word Hunts	✓	✓	✓	✓	✓	✓	✓	✓	✓	✓	✓	✓	✓	✓	✓	✓	✓	✓	✓	✓	✓	✓	✓
Making Big Words					✓	✓	✓	✓				✓	✓	✓	✓	✓	✓	✓	✓	✓	✓	✓	✓

Independent Application	Grade-Level Standards																						
	K				1							2						3				4	5
	a	b	c	d	a	b	c	d	e	f	g	a	b	c	d	e	f	a	b	c	d	a	a
Writing Center	✓	✓	✓	✓	✓	✓																	
Scaffolded Writing	✓	✓	✓	✓	✓	✓	✓	✓	✓	✓		✓	✓	✓	✓	✓	✓	✓	✓	✓	✓	✓	✓
Scaffolded Rereading	✓	✓	✓		✓	✓	✓	✓	✓	✓		✓	✓	✓	✓	✓	✓	✓	✓	✓	✓	✓	✓
Word Recording						✓			✓			✓	✓			✓	✓			✓	✓	✓	✓

The value of images declines as early as 3rd grade in curricular planning books. From *The Common Core Lesson Book, K-5* by Gretchen Owocki. Copyright © 2012 by Gretchen Owocki. Published by Heinemann, Portsmouth, NH. Reprinted by permission of the publisher. All rights reserved.

words: if I'm edu-sketching on the board while I'm explaining something, I typically don't have as many words. If I'm creating something for a handout, I'm more likely to use more written explanation, but it's still pithy. It's like taking a lump of clay and fashioning it into something more recognizable. One of the things my students tell me has been most useful about my sketches is the idea of seeing the whole puzzle put together, but with little pieces, or details, showing. Sometimes we use that to start from, and they can fill it in, or use it as a ready reference to complement their own notes.

We've already seen in Chapter 2 that our thinking is not linear, but reading is. Regardless of what language you speak, language usually follows a word order, as well as a storytelling order—often beginning, middle, and end. Our verbal brain, but not the visual brain, is attuned to this linear sequence. Although our brains have two hemispheres, with somewhat differing functions, they are both involved in the recognition and processing of language. Simple visuals belie their complexity as they tap into the whole brain and more accurately align with our thought patterns that circle back upon themselves to reconstruct understanding.

A NOD TO THE PAST

Let's go back. Way back.

We know that some of the earliest sketches on earth appear on the walls of caves. Replete with meaning, we have long supposed, but now researchers are paying attention to the symbols painted alongside the horses and bison. Scientists have identified 26 specific

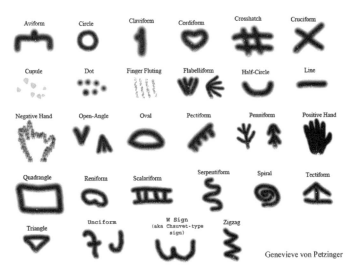

Aviform	Circle	Claviform	Cordiform	Crosshatch	Cruciform
Cupule	Dot	Finger Fluting	Flabelliform	Half-Circle	Line
Negative Hand	Open-Angle	Oval	Pectiform	Penniform	Positive Hand
Quadrangle	Reniform	Scalariform	Serpentiform	Spiral	Tectiform
Triangle	Unciform	W Sign (aka Chauvet-type sign)	Zigzag		

Genevieve von Petzinger

Symbols from the French Caves of Lascaux and Chauvet attest to the staying power of visuals. *Typology of Geometric Signs*, used with permission by Genevieve von Petzinger.

signs thought to be more than 30,000 years old in the French caves of Lascaux and Chauvet (considered to be twice as old as Lascaux).[6]

Recognize any of those symbols? The scientists actually found eerily similar symbols in caves continents apart, indicating a certain universality of representational thinking, since the artists could not have come in contact with each other. Fret not—if you have ever used any symbols similar to the ones above, you're not a thief. In the words of a seemingly chagrined Picasso following his visit to Lascaux: "We have invented nothing." You can almost hear his sigh. . . . Alas, Picasso is also credited with saying, "Good artists copy; great artists steal," implying that, hey, it's okay to take inspiration from others, and nothing is original anyway. That same sentiment is even written in the Bible to boot: "There is nothing new under the sun" (Ecclesiastes 1:9).[7] I'm going to use Austin Kleon's plea, "Steal like an artist"—embrace influence instead of running away with it, as you embark on your edu-sketching journey.[8] Draw inspiration from that which resonates with you, and make it your own. Share it with others, then share some more. In the end, we can all attribute our current-day visual notes to human emergence from the Ice Age.

Loath to call the cave symbols language or writing, scientists are cautiously intrigued by the patterns of symbol appearances in multiple locations from the same time period. One scientist goes so far as to surmise that our Cro-Magnon forbears were already comfort-

6 R. McKie, "Did Stone Age Cavemen Talk to Each Other in Symbols?," *The Observer*, March 10, 2012, http://www.theguardian.com/science/2012/mar/11/cave-painting-symbols-language-evolution.

7 A. Kleon, *Steal Like an Artist: 10 Things Nobody Told You About Being Creative* (New York: Workman, 2012). My only caveat here is that with edu-sketching, others' sketches will inspire and spur your thinking, but what's really important is the thinking behind the sketches—the process. And since visual note-takers are a fairly open and chummy lot, it pays to attribute credit whenever you can if you borrow someone else's signature style or symbology. There are many more resources than there used to be, with the explosion of social media and Internet sharing.

8 Ibid.

able with the use of these symbols, suggesting that they had been in use long before the cave paintings on materials less lasting.[9] The staying power of visual symbols is undeniable.

We see that it's not new for humans to rely heavily on visuals to comprehend the world around us. It's incredible to think we can perceive, draw, and imagine things we have never seen or experienced. That is the power of mental imagery. That is where innovation and invention come from. That is where curiosity and inspiration find their fuel (think Harry Potter's quidditch, Tolkien's Middle Earth, or Anne Frank's attic, for example). Why wouldn't we want to encourage our students to tap into this innate gift of thinking?

Studies have even demonstrated that blind individuals, who tend to capture their external world by touch, are able to reveal "internal representations through highly detailed drawings that are unequivocally understandable by a sighted person."[10] That's right—blind individuals have created detailed drawings of objects they have never physically seen, and they are accurate enough that you or I would know precisely what they were.

That, to me, is astounding.

This kind of feat highlights the fact that any level of accuracy depends on one's ability to construct, manipulate, and subsequently translate one's own mental representations in a stunning feat of cross-modal representation, the kind where information travels

between the tactile (touch) and the visual areas in the brain. But it's real. So here it is: the fact that merely touching something—thus encoding via tactile information—can spur mental representations even in people without sight is proof positive that there are few of us indeed who can accurately claim that they are not visual people.

WHERE HAVE ALL THE VISUALS GONE?

I'm blessed in that I have experienced teaching at all levels, K–12. I recently returned to teaching at the high school level, and my pressing question is, Where have all the visuals gone? What is it about getting older and its relationship to the credibility of using visuals in class? The big thrill of chapter books, that second grade point of pride of advancing to the level of chapter books, without so many pictures, because it's "grown-up"? Chapter books overrule picture books, and textbooks have incredibly dense texts that make it nearly impossible to pore over them and maintain interest. Of course, as you saw above, this isn't unique to high school; once students reach second or third grade, they are no longer asked to rely on pictures or to use them as a cornerstone of their expression.

No longer is language enhanced through pictures, because the emphasis is on the verbal, and the verbal is a single, linear, cognitive path—one way in, one way out. If we don't rehearse incoming information or link it to something memorable, it disappears. You know this if you've ever forgotten someone's name within minutes of meeting them. Repetition, repetition, repetition.

But why?

---

9 Genevieve von Petzinger, University of Victoria, British Columbia. March 2012. *Did Stone Age Cavemen Talk to Each Other in Symbols?* http://www.theguardian.com/science/2012/mar/11/cave-painting-symbols-language-evolution

10 Ibid.

Names, phone numbers, and, as you can imagine, bits of academic content—anything verbal or numerical—are dealt with by a system known as the phonological loop.[11] Within this loop are a phonological store, where incoming language is stored for about 2 seconds, and an articulatory control store, where linguistic information is rehearsed over and over.

There's also a visual-spatial sketchpad that takes care of what things look like, along with where we, and other objects, are in relation to each other. This is the place that lets us imagine objects, manipulate them in our minds to see various angles, and reconstruct them. Optical illusions are prime examples of how we can mentally manipulate objects and see something different each time we look at the same visual.

Then there's a central executive function which serves as the taskmaster and keeps track of what's going on in working memory. The thinking we do about concepts, objects, or people during edusketching is what gives it its mental mojo by helping make fragile memories into more enduring ones through attention, intention, and connections to previous knowledge. Allen Paivio posited a dual coding theory which states that the verbal system for language and the nonverbal visual-spatial system for images work in tandem for our thinking brains.[12] When we physically sketch images from or during our reading, incorporating our body into our work, both of these systems are tapped. There is an interplay between both hemispheres—that whole brain—as the abstract becomes more concrete. Paivio's research has shown that recall and recognition are enhanced by presenting information both verbally and visually, a fact that we seem to encounter over and over again.

But—and there are so many "buts"—at the same time, our brains, limited in capacity as they are, keep taking in new information. Just like a bathtub filling up with water, something's gotta give. Water, like new information, is added to the tub, to the point of overflowing. That new information merges with and reshapes the water it encounters, and sends a little back out so you can do something more with it—like store it again or forget about it. Thing is, the new water (information) is now intertwined with the old water (memories), and your memories that come out are not exactly like the ones you had encoded or stored. When it's hard to piece together lots of details, this is why. When your students confuse seemingly simple facts, this is why.

11 S. A. McLeod, "Working Memory," *Simply Psychology*, 2012, http://www.simplypsychology.org/working%20memory.html.

12 "Dual Coding Theory (Allan Paivio)," Instructional Design, accessed July 2014, http://www.instructionaldesign.org/theories/dual-coding.html.

One thing to note about these working memory systems is that they don't compete for attention—and this is critical for teachers. If someone has a PowerPoint presentation, and you are trying to listen while the presenter talks, it is nearly impossible to process both verbal inputs at once (effectively). Something's gotta give. Verbal and visual systems, however, do not compete with each other. You can view an image while listening to a speaker and process them simultaneously. They actually reinforce each other—which means we can maximize our time in the classroom, simply by increasing our reliance on visuals that supplement or enhance the verbal. Too much verbal, and we have a problem. Too much visual, and we also have a problem. Remember to combine the two for maximum effect—this includes talking while you're edu-sketching. Bring back the visuals!

How do you view your students' learning now?

ACTIVELY ENGAGE OUR VISUAL MINDS

One of the most powerful findings within the general category of instructional strategies is that graphic and symbolic representation of similarities and difference enhance students' understanding of content.

—*Robert Marzano,* Classroom Instruction That Works

Ever struggle to find the words to describe something—yet you can picture it with vast detail in your mind? Directions from here to your friend's house? A coveted outfit? That Norwegian landscape? Even if you know the words, the act of linking them together to give those visuals their verbal due just isn't quite enough. Our visual minds are powerful and continually trump the verbal, without us even realizing it.

We are surrounded by evidence that we should use more visuals in class:

- Of our entire sensory processing capacity, 75% is dedicated to vision.[13]
- Because we see with our brains, it makes sense that multisensory learning rocks.
- We know from neuroscience that visuals tap into multiple retrieval paths, and that when we remember an image, it's actually a reconstruction of knowledge in our memory from all those different pathways.
- When touch is combined with vision, learning jumps by up to 30% more than touch alone.[14]
- Images are processed 60,000 times faster than text.[15] This is because images are processed simultaneously and text is processed sequentially. This is why "glance media" asks whether your message can be processed effectively within 3 seconds.[16] Three seconds? That's crazy fast.

---

13 D. Roam, *Blah, Blah, Blah: What to Do When Words Don't Work* (New York: Penguin, 2011).

14 Medina, *Brain Rules.*

15 "Guides to Great Meetings: Wise Counsel: Polishing your presentation" 3M United States, http://www.3rd-force.org/meetingnetwork/readingroom/meetingguides.html.

16 L. Burmark, *They Snooze, You Lose* (San Francisco: Jossey-Bass, 2011).

- Over 90% of information transmitted to the brain is visual, yet 99% of all sensory information is filtered out by the brain almost immediately. Infographics are in that remaining 1%.[17] We are now a society that values information speed, pithiness, the reasons found in connections, and whatever holds our attention long enough to learn something from it.
- Psychologist Jerome Bruner of New York University has described studies showing that people only remember 10% of what they hear and 20% of what they read, but about 80 percent of what they see and do.[18]
- Yet other studies show that our learners will remember up to 55% more if we include a visual rather than relying on the spoken word alone. All kinds of people leverage this information to their advantage: lawyers know it, as do advertisers, branding specialists, and infographic creators. Even printer companies tout this information so you, too, can have astounding impact with your gorgeous visuals, since information with images is so superior in capturing attention.

Remember:

Fifty-five percent. Higher. Recall.

By adding a visual.

Isn't that worth tamping down your excuse that it "takes too

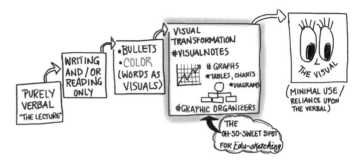

What combination of verbal and visual will work best to present your message or information?

much time" to include, find, or create visuals for class? (Despite the fact that letters and words are nothing more than symbols, which are pictures, we need imagery in class.) I might nearly guarantee that when you start thinking of ways to enter visual notes and imagery into your instruction, you will notice marked differences in both engagement and comprehension.

It's important to reiterate that these findings all point to the same conclusion—it's the combination of the visual and verbal that enhances learning. In case you want to know more about what works, Richard Mayer's "12 Principles of Multimedia Learning" chunks research findings into guidelines for better learning.[19] (Bonus: each has a fancy name to support what we already know.)

17 Mark Smiciklas, "Why Do Infographics Make Great Marketing Tools," Neo-Mam Studios, accessed November 2014, http://neomam.com/infographics-make-great-marketing-tools/. .

18 Paul Martin Lester, "Syntactic Theory of Visual Communication," California State University at Fullerton, 2006.

19 "12 Principles of Multimedia Learning," University of Hartford Faculty Center for Learning Development, accessed December 2014, http://hartford.edu

1. Display words and pictures together rather than successively (temporal contiguity principle).
2. Place corresponding words and pictures together (spatial contiguity principle).
3. Use graphics and voice narration instead of animation and on-screen text (modality principle). Remember, we can only tune into so much at once.
4. Use combined graphics and narration, but not graphics, narration, and on-screen text (Redundancy Principle). On-screen text is treated like competing visual imagery.
5. Chunk your instruction rather than blabbering on for long periods of time (segmenting principle).

You get the idea. Go check out his list, but here's the bottom line. People learn better from words and pictures than from words alone, also known as his multimedia principle.

Ebbinghaus would be impressed if we remembered that his curve of the same name also tells us much of our new information is gone—poof!—within the first hour after learning it, unless it's manipulated, applied, or accompanied by a visual. Consistent and increasingly elaborative review, such as sketching and then revisiting those sketches, perhaps to add more detail, is far more productive than cramming could ever be. Known as timed repetition, this approach is beneficial down to the neuronal level, as you learned in Chapter 2.

In spite of all this chatter about remembering and recall, forgetting is actually a useful aspect of our lives. Even though it may not always be exact, forgetting helps us prioritize what we pay attention to. If we remembered everything we've ever learned, well . . . talk about a mess in our minds. Our brains are pretty good at pruning, just like gardening. Imagine trimming tiny dendritic neuron hedges with pruning shears. What's no longer used, what hasn't been activated for awhile, can be pruned. Once we know how to walk, or to add 2 plus 2, those learning pathways can be replaced with new ones. And yes, even what we think we remember may be forgotten, thanks to the way our brains reconstruct memories every time we call them forward and store them again.

One of the greatest advantages of edu-sketching is for students to have time to reflect, connect, and consolidate learning. Even 2 or 3 minutes of sketching interspersed throughout class time promotes memory encoding—maybe sketch a new vocabulary word or key figure. Sketching doesn't need to be complex, and plenty of studies show that images too lifelike or complex can be distracting. (Chapter 5 provides more detail about an intriguing phenomenon related to lifelike images, called the uncanny valley.) What matters is letting our visual capacity come out and play so it can nurture and create those multiple neural pathways of access. Students learn in so many different ways; sketching provides artistic opportunities for students to express their understanding without getting hung up on the words. If your goal is to reach all students, it's critical to include student-generated visual imagery.

/academics/faculty/fcld/data/documentation/technology/presentation/powerpoint/12_principles_multimedia.pdf.

IF IT WORKS FOR ADULTS

Ever been in a meeting where, ahem, someone loved to hear himself talk? We're so accustomed to relying on words to clarify and explain, but what if you knew that using sketches in business meetings—yes, with adults—especially interactive sketches, "shortens meeting times by 24%" and that "visual language aids the decision-making process"? Sixty-four percent of participants make decisions after seeing visual displays. But that's not all—charts and posters help "anchor ideas and keep concepts alive long after the meeting."[20] In my experience, larger-scale edu-sketching, the ones where I take up the board and continue to add information, organizes information into meaningful patterns and brings the big picture into focus. Adults and students alike can start discovering what goes together and how items relate. Words from the speaker tend to live a little longer when they're on paper for others to see. That's the type of know-how, confident understanding, and solution finding we want to harness in our classrooms.

According to businesses, then, sketching helps engage more people, enhances understanding of the content, and hastens decision making, all while appeasing the visual learning modality. In my experience, that's all true. I've also experienced that sketches promote questioning and commenting, which in turn shows deeper thought during and after reading or listening. Discussions are spurred, dialogues provoked, and laughter is prompted. In tandem, interest rockets skyward. At the very least, sketches encourage another look at the content, which is a gift in itself for any span of classroom engagement.

If I'm drawing while eliciting others' thoughts, my audience always want to make sure I've interpreted them accurately, and that's been with adults and children. We all love being heard. Being drawn and quoted (sounds alarmingly like "drawn and quartered"—now there's a visual) resonates with us as listeners and literally draws us further into the conversation. There are masterful dynamics with edu-sketching in the mix or at the center.

Considering all that simple sketches have done for business-people,[21] and how much they have done for my classroom, you can see how it's not just drawing in class. It's about the process. Process over pretty also means that the end justifies the means. Edu-sketching is not the end-all, but it can be an effective tool in getting to the end result—deeper understanding.

Visual notes provide fodder for a happy brain, the organ that thrives on piecing things together, finding patterns, associating, and assigning meaning to even the most abstract of visuals. Visual notes can become a higher-level anchor chart, if you will, one that serves as a continual reference point. It's also an interactive living document, always inviting more connections, additions, and changes.

---

20 Mille Sonnemon, "Facilication," Hands on Graphics, accessed December 2014, http://www.handsongraphics.com/facilication.htm.

21 If you're a meeting junkie or, better yet, an anti-meeting junkie, check out Sunni Brown's Doodle Revolution (http://sunnibrown.com/doodlerevolution/) for some amazing ideas to try if you ever have to make a group decision. Dan Roam's *Blah-Blah-Blah: What to Do When Words Don't Work* also has some fantastic tools "to help us combine our visual and verbal minds."

Food for thought, too—for those of you with hearing-impaired or deaf students in your classes, imagine how sketches can enhance their comprehension, involvement, and interest.

POWER OF VISUALS

The mind sees what it wants and can overpower the rational or, at times, the physical. Imagination is a powerful form of visualization. Vaclav Havel noted that the drawings from the children of Terezin concentration camp in the Czech Republic held "only a shadow of grief and anxiety in them. There is much more about dreams of spring, of flowers, butterflies, birds, and also a great longing to be happy and carefree."[22] Out of approximately 15,000 children that were in the camp from 1942 to 1944, only about 100 are estimated to have survived. The children used their drawings as a defense, an emotional release, and a vehicle for their dreams. Even the simplest sketches were powerful enough to remain "an expressive testimony" for us in the 21st century. Those children were able to express visceral and complex ideas, with words and pictures, directly from their hearts. The power of a single image, hand drawn, snakes through to the heart, the mind, and the memory. Just like that.

Physiological response to simple visuals also occurs with far less emotional information, thanks to what are known as "networks of

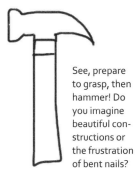

See, prepare to grasp, then hammer! Do you imagine beautiful constructions or the frustration of bent nails?

representation."[23] Information is stored in more than one region of the brain—via sound, feelings, smells, sensations, and so on. Looking at a sketch of a hammer propels your motor neurons to prepare to grasp and subsequently hammer—without having moved a conscious muscle. It has to simultaneously activate neurons in your visual processing system, too, because that's where it tells you what it is, links to the word "hammer," and probably conjures up sounds, finished construction projects, and, in my case, a bit of throbbing pain in my thumb. Again, this exemplifies the gamut of associations that arise from a single, simple image.

Mental rehearsal is used by many athletes to improve their physical performance when they imagine performing certain tasks with ideally positive outcomes.[24] Interestingly, functional MRI brain imaging during this mental rehearsal shows an actual shift in activity from the left hemisphere to the right.[25] Since the right hemisphere is believed to be more involved in holistic and creative thinking, while the left handles the more logical, this shift from the logical to the

22 Vaclav Havel was a notable Czech president. Vaclav Havel, afterword to *I Never Saw Another Butterfly: Children's Drawings and Poems from Terezin Concentration Camp, 1942–1944* (New York: Schocken, 1994).

23 F. Bailey and K. Pransky, *Memory at Work in the Classroom* (Alexandria, VA: ASCD, 2014).

24 David R. McDuff, *Sports Psychiatry: Strategies for Life Balance and Peak Performance* (Washington, DC: American Psychiatric Publishing; 2012), 41–42.

25 Ibid.

creative is what enhances visual imagery and, thus, performance. For me, this is useful information because it demonstrates the direct link between what we and our students envision and what we can do. Another scientist notes that visualization also creates stronger neural patterns in the brain which can improve neuromuscular coordination and, hence, movement—evidence that conscious visualization is equally engaging for the brain and its myriad connections throughout the body.[26]

THE MEMORY PALACE

Hooks. Visual ones. That's what makes our memories stick. Just ask Simonides. Or, heck, be like him—the ancient, but alive version. Partygoer extraordinaire, as poets were wont to be back in the day, Simonides had just finished reciting at a gathering and had stepped outside. Within minutes, the building crumbled to the ground, killing all guests inside and disfiguring them to the point of unrecognizability. After closing his eyes and contemplating for a few minutes, Simonides took each of the distraught relatives by the hand and led them to their kin.

He did this by associating each person with his physical location in the room through reconstructive visualization. Using the "memory palace" technique of recall, he associated strikingly vivid imagery with each memory, then mentally walked himself through the building. "At that moment," Joshua Foer writes in his memoir *Moon-*

walking with Einstein, "according to legend, the art of memory was born."[27]

The key elements of the art of memory are the use of mental images and their placement in ordered, often architectural, settings. It wasn't just used by the Greeks, either. Roman schools of rhetoric took this practice a step further, creating a practical system with students memorizing interiors of large buildings and dividing their spaces into specific "loci" (places) to which they attached information to remember.[28]

This works because we know our minds recall images more readily than ideas; the more vivid and emotionally charged, the better, and the order of a piece within a given context counts on your chains of association to resonate. In short, strong visuals have the ability to make learning stick. Whenever possible, attach an image to your words. Even simple images can grab attention, though—so don't discount anything. Start with the basics because that will at least engage more widespread areas of the brain, ideally leading you to the big picture. Finessing the details can come later. Remember the visual hooks.

---

26 K. Porter, *The Mental Athlete* (Champaign, IL: Human Kinetics, 2004).

27 J. Foer, *Moonwalking with Einstein: The Art and Science of Remembering Everything* (New York: Penguin, 2011).

28 I'd certainly suggest reading Joshua Foer's book (ibid.) about his own memory championship experiences, as well as Lewis Smile, *The Memory Palace: Learn Anything and Everything (Starting with Shakespeare and Dickens)* (Author, 2012). Smile's book walks you through Shakespeare's plays in chronological order with memorable specific examples.

THE McGURK EFFECT

The McGurk effect is another demonstration that what you see even influences what you hear.[29] Think of dubbed films. What you see clashes with what you hear and can override what speakers are saying. Mouth movements can influence what we think we're hearing. The effect is bizarre, and even when you know what's happening, it doesn't seem to make a difference. You think you hear the sound the speaker's lips are making. We rely on lip-reading far more than we realize. Watching head movements in general helps us distinguish sentence beginnings and endings, even through eyebrow movements.

When we struggle to understand, whether due to language learning or background noise, our gaze naturally shifts to the speaker's mouth. We are, in essence, speech readers. If you have ever learned another language, you have probably experienced this firsthand. It's always very challenging (and nerve-racking!) for me to talk in another language to someone over the phone, even if it's someone who understands my version of their language. The first time this happened stirred a great realization within me of how much I relied on lip-reading and facial expression to comprehend context and appropriate reactions, and even to determine the end of their sentences. Our students, unbeknownst to them, do the same thing as they're watching us. This effect attests to how our senses work together, how they share and influence each other, without any conscious effort of ours. It also attests to the incredible power of our mind's eye.

Not only is there a lot more going on inside our learners than we could impart from the outside (i.e., teachers), but we also take a lot for granted in our learning. No wonder our lessons need to be more than verbal.

EMPHASIZE THE REASON WHY

Children naturally connect thoughts, words, and images long before they master the skill of writing. There's a word for it, too, this act of snagging meaning from multiple symbol systems and switching back and forth from one to another: transmediation. If we write down an idea or some content, we think about it one way; but if we sketch the same information, we automatically think about it in a new or different way. With both on paper, we can compare and refine, going back and forth until our understanding is distilled to its essence. It's practical for students to understand this innate ability.

When we emphasize the use of art, whether students view art or create their own, they interweave new ideas and information from their own knowledge and background experiences to produce their own narratives. Encouraging students to observe, interpret, and then create helps us and our students generate ideas and organize thoughts. As a result, we communicate more effectively. The clearer the picture, the clearer the understanding. Engage students via multiple pathways like this to enhance learning—and create multiple retrieval paths to boot. Hook into baseline background knowledge

---

29 For a great explanation of the McGurk effect, watch this video: BBC Two, "Try the McGurk Effect! Horizon: Is Seeing Believing?," November 10, 2010, https://www.youtube.com/watch?v=G-lN8vWm3m0.

and manipulate connections in that trove of knowledge tucked in our long-term memory.

Tapping into these multiple symbol systems helps learners find connections and relationships. Ask kids if they've studied their linear notes—and more than likely, the response will be in the negative. You can change that.

We know the brain loves repetition, and we know that frequent note review over a longer period of time is what helps learning stick . . . but if kids aren't interested in rereading their notes, or motivated to take them in the first place, it's a moot point. For older students, it takes some convincing that pictures aren't just for little kids. Weave in some history about Egyptian hieroglyphics, cave paintings, and fascinating oracle bone pictographs of China to nudge their understanding of the history of how others have used pictures for communication. Tell them about rebuses, runes, petroglyphs, and optical illusions. Talk about architects and engineers and even graphic novelists or cartoonists. Look at advertising—whether in print or elsewhere—to consider the effectiveness of simple sketches and what elements are most memorable.

Talk about perceptual ambiguity. Look at an object together, but from different vantage points in the room to demonstrate how there is more than one frame of reference. Or look at an optical illusion. Sometimes it's easy to miss the point unless we are oriented by a suggestion or particular focus. Often a reorientation helps us view the image in a whole new way.[30] Sometimes, if you're like me, it's difficult to go back to the original view you held. Just like the opti-

cal illusion here—as my brain switches between seeing an old woman and younger girl, sometimes I have a hard time finding one or the other without a suggestion. (Reorientation for you: the younger woman's chin is the old woman's nose.)

Keep that in mind and relate it to your instruction—the fact that we can be reoriented by someone else's suggestion to shift our focus. How often do we reorient students' thinking through our suggestions? How often do we mean to do that, and how is our students' learning influenced?

Talk to them about the brain, the reason behind visual note-taking. Remind them that their working memory can only hold so much information at a time, even when faced with torrents of information daily. If information lacks meaning for us, individually speaking, it will most likely be forgotten. Alas, not all information we impart will be meaning-

I don't know about you but I need a "reference point" to rediscover the original image and focus each time I try to find both women in this image. This image, often referred to as "Boring figure," has been widely attributed to British cartoonist W. E. Hill, who published it in 1915. Later, its appearance was evidenced as early as 1888 and 1890. It has since been altered and tweaked by several artists and psychologists.

ful to our students, and that means sometimes we all need to be conscious about how to make it so. Call it a life skill.

Edu-sketching is not something you can force any of your students to do, but provide opportunities for your visual and verbal sides to intermingle and see what happens.

---

30 Candice Jones Peelman, "Optical Illusions," Cincibility, May 17, 2013, https://cincibility.files.wordpress.com/2013/05/old-woman-young-woman.gif.

ICONS AND SYMBOLS

Vision is not enough; it must be combined with venture. It is not enough to stare up the steps; we must step up the stairs.
—*Vaclav Havel, progressive Czech author and politician*

Speaking of big pictures and finessing details, I believe we under-estimate how often we make meaning through the use of abstrac-tions, so let's take a look at icons and symbols in our world. Given the age of apps and symbols, infographics, and increasingly linguistically diverse societies, it's a necessary skill for our students to become flu-ent in both text and imagery. Visual literacy must include not only "reading" nonlinguistic symbols, but also "writing" or creating them, not only reading between others' visual lines, but also creating equally provocative images of our own.

Icons are simple images similar to the shape they represent, which makes them nearly instantly recognizable, like a printer image or pencil for editing within your computer toolbar. Symbols are images whose meaning must be learned, such as the bald eagle for America or a cross for Christianity. There may not be any really visi-ble resemblance to the object they represent, and they may be very personal or culturally grounded. As you edu-sketch, some symbols may even be generated when you're in your classroom while dis-cussing a specific topic—a type of shorthand to represent what you are learning together.

The brain loves patterns and as such, it's going to seek out pat-terns even when you don't try to. Some patterns have been there the whole time, and we just needed to take the time to look for them.

Some symbols are more universal than others, representing thought patterns that have endured through time and across borders. Water, for example, easily depicted as

Several different symbols for water have been found worldwide, yet they are still recognizable.

is often linked to birth, purification, and rebirth or rejuvenation, while circles or rings might symbolize unity.[31]

Edu-sketching is an ideal vehicle for comparing literal and sym-bolic meaning, for example, the word "ancient" was signified by a spiderweb for one student, an Egyptian pyramid for another, and a pirate ship for yet another student. Each was symbolic and opened up discussion we would otherwise have missed; plus they opened little windows into their minds for me. Often, writing itself is what helps sort through ideas, and sketching pictures falls directly into the same camp. This is one reason teachers in elementary school always tell their students to make movies in their mind before they begin writing. High schoolers and middle schoolers should do the same.

As you encourage your students to sketch, it's helpful to remind them first about process over pretty—it's not an art contest. This is about the process more than anything. Remind them, too, that

---

31 J. Suler, "Symbolism: What Does It Mean?," *Photographic Psychology: Image and Psyche*, 2013, http://users.rider.edu/~suler/photopsy/symbolism.htm.

when people look at their edu-sketches, they are apperceptive, and will respond intuitively to any universal meaning they can attach to it. Apperception helps us make sense of something by associating it with ideas and thoughts we already have. Symbols and icons help us with this association, hence making connections that become priceless for helping retrieve our thoughts. Reminding students about others' apperception (and yes, teach them that word), is a gift. If students feel more comfortable using words, phrases, or even short sentences, then by all means allow them to, in conjunction with their sketches.

To quell further student angst, toss some information their way about universal patterns and images, what Carl Jung, a famous psychological theorist, called archetypes. These are the kinds of images we respond instinctively to, whether we realize it or not. How we interpret these images, of course, depends on the viewer's background and understanding, but the automaticity is impressive. We can go back to the example of water and its many representations. Or we can look at this to see how rapidly our minds piece information together:

Those of us who read the Roman alphabet recognize the bottom half of our letters because they are integral pieces of information in our life. Same with fonts—although different, we can still read them.

We are constantly on the lookout for something recognizable because that is what resonates most deeply, even when we desire novelty.

Connect, associate, make relevant. Sound familiar?

METAPHORS

Look at items in your own surrounding. Can you see a weapon, an animal, a nightmare, or a poem represented in that spoon or cell phone on the table? Ignite your imagination the way a child does.
—*Rick Wormelli,* Metaphors and Analogies: Power Tools for Teaching Any Subject

Admit it. You've done it at least once in your lifetime. You've pretended a banana was a telephone. Or you've at least personified a sun by adding a face to it. Simple play, or so you think. More likely, you didn't think about it at all. You were making sense of the world through what is known as metaphorical representation. (Teach that phrase to your 3-year-old.)

Think about all the symbols we so easily recognize—pi, the Christian cross, an American flag. Most discussions distinguish symbols from metaphors because they are more permanent, perhaps more ubiquitous in given cultures, and are typically shown as images. Metaphors are more linguistic, representing ideas and images using words rather than images themselves, yet they invoke strong mental imagery that aids comprehension and understanding.

Some may feel that symbols are superfluous or too stereotypical, or that metaphors are mere flashes of insight and not as lasting.

Others may feel that they would each be better represented in some other way. Regardless, our reliance upon symbolic thinking and the use of metaphors in everyday life is habitual and something no longer in our conscious approach to the world and its ideas. James Geary, legendary aphorist and author, attests to this in his TED Talk;[32] he claims we utter about six metaphors a minute.

Archetypal symbols carry the same (similar) meanings in a near-universal sense, such as "Mother" earth, light, up-down, an axis of a wheel, and the circle. They appear in multiple cultures, many remote and distant from each other—enough to preclude thoughts that they even communicated with each other. This demonstrates the natural inclination for humans to associate one thing with another and to share that meaning with others.

Think for a moment how deeply word usage and word choice impart and impact symbolic meaning. Here are some examples. How would you sketch Column 1? Column 2? How easily do images come to mind for each column?

The queen rules over her country.	The queen rules under her country.

The family fell into hard times.	The family climbed into hard times.
She's cool.	She's hot.
The information shed light on the problem.	The information shed darkness on the problem.

These are all examples of metaphorical language, readily understood words and phrases. The word "light" used to carry connotations of both intellectual light and the "warmth of enthusiasm" that goes with it.[33] Now, intellectual light is commonly represented by

32 J. Geary, "Metaphorically Speaking," TED Global, July 2009, http://www.ted.com/talks/james_geary_metaphorically_speaking?language=en.

33 P. Wheelwright, *Metaphor and Reality* (Bloomington: Indiana University Press, 1962).

symbols such as a lightbulb or an illuminated exclamation point, but it's not unusual to talk about the fire that lights our imaginations and stirs our soul. How ingrained are some of these ideas in your mind? How difficult or easy was it for you to conjure imagery for these? And what about that next step of actually sketching out your thoughts? Can you see the value of providing time for information to marinate in your students' minds?

The use of metaphor in language is well known, but it's also extensive in visual art. Visual metaphors are images used instead of words to represent a comparison. They are thought to be understood by the right hemisphere long before the more literal-minded left hemisphere can spell out the reasons. It all goes back to that wickedly fast processing of visuals in our brain. Art seems to dissolve the barriers between the hemispheres, weaving the left hemisphere's language-based logic with the more holistic and intuitive thinking associated with the right hemisphere.

Synesthetic metaphors also shed light on how our senses are hardwired to integrate their information. Synesthesia is a fascinating mingling of our senses. Some people might taste lemon when they touch metal or taste earwax when they hear someone's name. Others might associate textures with colors, or see colors when they hear numbers or letters. I see the months of the year in a certain pattern (a curved L shape, if you must know), with certain colors for each month and for each day of the year. Same with numbers. Before thinking that's strange, consider how many of our metaphors are synesthetic, because you might be a synesthete, too. After all, everything in our brain is more and more likely connected to everything else. (Remember those "cross-modal" connections?)

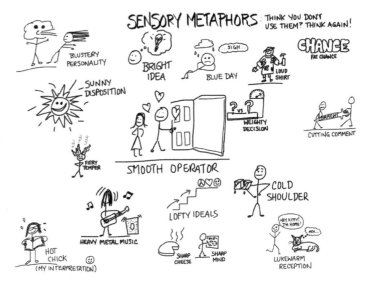

IDIOMS

An idiom is a group of words used together in a phrase or saying, the holistic meaning of which is very different from each of the words on its own. They're a conundrum to language learners and native speakers alike, sometimes even aptly called "presolved little cryptic word puzzles."[34] One telltale cognitive sign of idioms is that they are pre-

34 J. Bhalla, *I'm Not Hanging Noodles on Your Ears and Other Intriguing Idioms From Around the World* (Washington, DC: National Geographic Society, 2009).

packaged bits of information—remember how the brain loves chunking? Well, idioms answer that need for chunking quite nicely; the brain considers words and idioms as lexemes, which are self-contained units for conveying meaning. What heightens the complexity of the idioms is the fact that the words together hold a very different meaning from the words on their own.

"Paying an arm and a leg" for a television set doesn't reduce you to a mere torso, sans extremities. In the United States I will know that you paid more than you feel was necessary, and in Spain, "your tongue may be hanging out like a man's tie," as you'd be exhausted from working too much to pay for it.

Dissecting those phrases, "paid an arm and a leg" and "your tongue may be hanging out like a man's tie," makes it easy to see how comprehending idioms is a complex cognitive challenge. First you read the individual words, then you realize they make up a greater lexeme, or meaningful unit, and in turn, you interpret the phrase as a whole. They do lend themselves to some pretty vivid mental images, though.

Researchers have found differences in processing time between literal and idiomatic phrases and have found that the brain definitively uses both hemispheres when interpreting figurative language. Although they share the processing wealth, the right hemisphere may be more involved in evaluating and comprehending idiomatic meaning, whereas the left hemisphere may play a greater role in the emotional connotation of idiomatic language.

Knowing now what we do about the hunger of the visual areas of the brain and how critical it is to keep them fed, it makes clear sense to emphasize the power of visuals and visualization for teaching.

Renowned word linguist David Crystal tells us that nearly two-thirds of jokes depend on some sort of word play[35]—and we know that the brain thrives on novelty with a touch of surprise. This might explain the popularity of the use of idioms, metaphors, and other figurative language. Idioms and figurative language are universal, found in many languages—and reading phrases such as these are linguistic windows into other cultures. Figurative language provides some of the most brilliant ideas for edu-sketching, too, as a jumping-off point for our artistic journey.

Just as we consume gourmet food to generate complex taste and texture experiences for our gastronomic pleasure, Ramachandran considers art as gourmet food for the visual centers in the brain.[36] It doesn't have to be gorgeous, breathtaking or award-winning, either—remember the power of the process for your students.

Have students read an idiom and sketch what they think it means, then use the idiom in context, determine the true meaning, and have them re-sketch again. Simple activity, but guaranteed laughter will help cement the learning!

35 D. Crystal, *Language Play* (Chicago: University of Chicago Press, 1998).
36 Ramachandran, *The Tell-Tale Brain*.

Even younger students can understand the concept of metaphors and make connections to their own lives and experiences. With a little bit of fun!

VISUAL RESONANCE

Visual resonance, or "echo," refers to the resonance between a concept in a word and the way the word is represented, for example, a printed word "tilt" that is literally tilted, or "dizzy" with its letters all ajumble, blurring the boundary between conception and perception. Sometimes called typographic resonance, it combines imagery with typography. The word is still legible, and the meaning or idea of the word is illustrated. Maybe "scary" or "shiver" is printed in wiggly lines as if they were themselves trembling. Maybe Antarctica is written in "icy" letters. The effectiveness of this type of visual acts as a sort of echo of your own shiver—which in turn resonates with the concept of fear. Seeing a word like "fear" in haunted, wiggly letters rather than plain old manuscript print might lend instant background to your reading and get your heart pumping. Playing around with letters and typography may be a comfortable entry point for your students, so it's useful to show some examples. Better yet, create some examples with them.

The point here is that when we think, we visualize. We imagine.

We merge the symbolic with the linguistic, in so many ways, and we create visual metaphors in our mind. We use visual metaphors far more than we realize. Edu-sketching taps into that visual thinking and draws it out. Symbols and drawings can actually be metaphors, conveying information and substituting one thing for another. Meaning starts to extend well beyond the image or symbol, and reinterprets thoughts in ways that merge analysis with art. Ah, the sweet smell of synthesis.

One of the most entrenched misconceptions of edu-sketching is that it is not mentally rigorous. Some may refer to it as "drawing pictures in class" or "making cartoons." It is deceptively challenging, which is why our students will benefit. Your thinking differs in both engagement and accountability when you merely think fleeting thoughts versus tangibly sketching to demonstrate your thinking. That previous metaphor exercise? One word can impact the entire meaning of a sentence. You can think "that's nice," or, "of course I know the difference" but until you literally try to sketch it, your full thinking is not optimized. You start manipulating images in your mind and reconnecting to experiences or previously learned knowledge to find that "best fit" for a sketch to make sense. Yes, it takes more time, but it also strengthens memory.

And for those who claim art has no place in the content-area classroom, challenge them to a duel. It would be a draw.

Besides, Pope Gregory said it was okay to make art, and that was a long, long time ago. I just happen to agree. Plus, it's fabulous exercise for our right hemisphere. And left.

Ask your students, regardless of their age, to make movies in their mind, to create mental pictures and images as they read, listen, and otherwise engage with texts. Their mental pictures make it personal, hence memorable, and we experience that effect ourselves when immersed in a good book. Such mental images recruit their own background knowledge, with multisensory information to make mental pictures all the richer.

Drawing those mental pictures, however—both literally and figuratively—is not easy, and your students will need guidance to get started. Be prepared not only to model but to ask guiding questions: "Based on what you know so far, how could we represent this (character, element, event, vocabulary word, etc.) in a sketch or visual? What details are the most important to include? Which details help us understand the (context, feelings, emotion, urgency, etc.) in your visual?" Chapters 4 and 5 will have plenty of examples for your classroom.

I urge you to seek figurative language and patterns, and to create icons and illustrations together with your students in various content areas. Determine which symbols and sketches most appropriately capture topics or common concepts, and encourage different versions of the same ideas. Creating these together can not only help create a common language, but also help foster community and trust.

MIRROR NEURONS

Speaking of creating together, let's talk a little about the role of mirror neurons. These are the neurons that automatically simulate an equivalent action in your imagination, but that's not all. They also take that simulation one step further and help muscles produce the same action they "think" someone else is about to do. Watch people engaged in conversations: people unconsciously mirror each other's body postures and language. When I've witnessed this and mentioned it to people later, most of them never realized they were doing any such thing.

What on earth does that mean for teachers? Well, in the classroom, a simple example could be that when we grab a whiteboard marker and face the whiteboard, students' mirror neurons automatically form assumptions and anticipate that we will write or sketch something. You've also seen it before, when a student responds to your question, then searches your face for a reaction—then changes his response accordingly. When learning language, we watch others' lip movements to determine how to say something or clarify what is being said. Babies and children are expert mirrors (sometimes). Some consider mirror neurons as "central to social learning, imitation, and the cultural transmission of skills and attitudes" thanks to the imitative learning associated to them.[37]

Mirror neurons may also explain the mysterious effects we experience during reading, that holy grail time when words are experienced as if we were acting them out ourselves, that time when we are utterly absorbed in our book. Reading is active engagement with a text and its ideas, and research has shown that neural circuits change as we read, whenever we think about thoughts from someone else's mind. Some would even say that language is not just comprehended, but experienced, and the reader becomes the book.[38] (Now there's a metaphor for you.) The importance of interaction in

---

37 Ibid., Kindle ed., location 628/6232.

38 J. Davis, The Reader Organisation, "Why Reading Matters," part of the BBC4 Why Reading Matters Series. video link: https://www.youtube.com/watch

learning is undeniable, but so is the inter- and intraplay of our thoughts.

The existence of the mirror neuron system also helps explain why sometimes you need to jump right in to learn a new skill, to risk making mistakes, rather than hanging back to watch your teacher until you think you have it. Here's what is interesting, though—watching before you try means that you will probably see very little; watching after you try something new will engage the mirror system, increasing your brain's power to get it.

Neuroscientists explain this phenomenon by comparing it to tennis: apparently when you look at something you've done or experienced before, "you are actually using more of your brain to see it, so there's a richer information flow. Until you started playing tennis, you couldn't see the difference between a good topspin stroke and a bad one; after a few weeks of practice, when your coach demonstrates the stroke, you really get it visually. And you can thank the mirror system for that."[39] From this thinking we can easily rationalize the idea of jumping right into edu-sketching with our students: anticipate their initial hesitancy, but also expect them to be able to meet your expectations. Don't worry if they copy your sketches at first—that's normal. Just encourage them to tweak, then create their own a bit at a time, since more learning comes from the process.

?v=ml3FzgvaiDQ, accessed November 2014. J. Davis, Personal Blog "readerjane davis" https://readerjanedavis.wordpress.com/

39 Jon Spayde, *6 Surprising Things That Affect Your Brain*, Care2, http://www.care2.com/greenliving/6-surprising-things-that-affect-your-brain.html.

As you consider building lessons, or parts of your lessons, around visuals, keep in mind the role of these mirror neurons—some students will benefit from watching you edu-sketch before they try it themselves. But others will benefit from trying it first, then watching. This process is ripe for metacognitive awareness, by the way.

WAIT TIME AND REFLECTION

Wait time is automatically built in and extended when kids edu-sketch in class. This much needed wait time, or time after the teacher asks a question, helps kids reflect and think about content they've just heard. The typical length of wait time we use is less than a second, which then leads kids to short recall-type responses. Extending that wait time up to 7–8 seconds allows students to formulate their thinking into more critical and nuanced responses. We as educators really need to embrace the silence after we ask a question—let students process and mentally visualize, then sketch. It helps when your prompt is pertinent and predetermined. There are better places than others to stop and synthesize in a text or during a lecture (SASSy points)—some content is much more intriguing or conceptually accessible to kids. Sometimes you may want them to make a supported prediction or inference, and a sketch may be just the prime their brains need. Know your audience and tweak the time available in class.

Allowing time for thinking to percolate, for thoughts to be more articulate and clear, means allowing time for reflection—throughout the lesson as well as at the end. Honestly? Building in reflection time is one of the most challenging things I do in my classes on a consistent basis, but edu-sketching provides that time inherently for us. The time to sketch, to really see or understand the content, is time for introverts, struggling learners, language learners, and others to be successful, rather than be left out when the extroverts synthesize and respond much more quickly.

Another tip from my experience? Sometimes if we want deeper reflection, it's appropriate to make sharing something optional.

Brazilian educator Paolo Friere says this about reflection and its essential role in learning—and its role for learners becoming world change agents, those who can transform the world: "Within the word we find two dimensions, reflection and action, in such radical interaction that if one is sacrificed—even in part—the other immediately suffers."[40] Of course, any shared reflection demands trust, and Freire further notes the essence of dialogue, with its value being grounded in humility, mutual trust, and, yes, love. In other words, reflection at its best is grounded in the relationships with our students and our shared sense of classroom community.

Rather than letting reflection become the most neglected part of our instruction, an occurrence left to the last hurried minutes of class, remember to build it in daily. Taking the time to edu-sketch, whether as a class or individually, lets teachers and students really see and understand what has been taught, and synthesize what has

been learned. Those precious moments that typically disappear after learning? Take the time to save them.

A Quick Note on Different Styles

Note-taking like this doesn't have a set style, which is yet another beauty of its wide-ranging appeal. Think of it as a visual language, with multiple dialects, and mutual comprehensibility—albeit with slightly different presentations. Accents and vocabulary, if you will. How you choose to represent the concept of innovation may differ from another, in relation to your background, experiences, and what resonates most deeply with you, as exemplified earlier with the word "house."

MOVIES IN YOUR MIND

I've mentioned more than once that many educators ask their students to make movies in their mind as they read or as they listen to a text. No matter what you do, you are likely to form images in your head. How many times have you lamented the fact that a movie version of a book just wasn't as good? Or if you are about to attend your school's homecoming dance, you imagine the clothing, music, lighting, faces of friends you hope will be there (or not), and so on. Your mind creates fantastic mini-movie versions constantly. Creating a mental picture of events taking place in a story—and predicting what may or may not happen next—aids comprehension and helps

---

40 P. Freire, *Pedagogy of the Oppressed*, 30th anniversary ed. (New York: Bloomsbury, 2012), 88.

students remember the main idea with details. How do we make the best use of this visualization strategy?

Textbooks are incredibly dense texts, especially at the middle and high school levels. Whether or not they can be accessed digitally is a moot point; what's striking is how dry they can be, in either format. Take a history book, for example. Stuffed with facts, maybe a smattering of helpfully interesting drawings or photos, but very little storytelling or room to imagine what life was really like. Although sidebars and photos are meant to supplement the many facts, students must constantly be reminded to read them, as if they were distracting from the meat of the text—which aren't typically inviting, or accessible to many struggling readers, in the first place. (Sorry, textbook authors—just calling it like I see it.) In this time of unprecedented access to information, textbooks are no longer the sole source of content information.

When embarking on a new topic area, I amass images from the Internet and my personal collection, as well as an armload of picture books from the library to help enhance kids' interest. The images and book illustrations draw them in; unbeknownst to the students, they are absorbing informative details that supplement the text itself. Students begin making connections almost instantaneously. Picture book authors are unconstrained by the need to fill each page with facts, and their books can be replete with expressive language and rich imagery. The combination of reduced amounts of text alongside the images does not diminish its academic value by any means. Even wordless books can be equally powerful, leveling the comprehension playing field when students analyze and infer from pictures alone. These books are actually great tools for determining what makes a good visual, what's a good amount of information to include and a good amount to leave to the reader's imagination.

The point of all this is that even images like simple sketches draw people in. A sketch drawn during a presentation will draw far more onlookers than a transcript posted nearby. People will linger, thinking about what the images represent, what the artist was thinking when she used a particular drawing to represent an idea, and maybe even wonder how they themselves would have sketched the same topic. Inferences and ideas stem from myriad perspectives and perceptions, but also—and this is key—questions. Many topics are very advanced, and the simplest of picture books can actually be critical to our students learning to read or improve their reading.

Reliance on pictorial clues to promote and deepen comprehension is nothing new. What I'm asking now is that we take the images from our students' thinking and lend them credence and value at a time when we rely heavily on other visual images in our world. We can do this through edu-sketching and by asking them continually, "How would you represent this?" "What does this mean?" "How would you change it if . . . ?" and simply, "What if . . . ?" as they begin drawing at SASSy points, to stop and synthesize.

Edu-sketching, as you understand by now, is ideal for integrating prior and new knowledge, as a springboard to a new topic, a means of prediction, or as a stretch assignment to add more details to support your case. Sharing imagery with others extends our learning as we discover details that were important to others. In my class, when we share our sketches, most students will share the main idea, but have differing details. This makes students think more deeply about why their peers chose those details. It reminds them of details they may have forgotten or skimmed over, and I know it is engaging because students love to question each other's thinking through their sketches.

Creating movies and pictures in our minds as we read requires careful attention, and often rereading. Students have noticed as we read that certain words evoke stronger imagery than others—which in turn provides a teachable moment about how writers choose their words carefully in order to do just that. Sketching images also makes reviewing information more tangible—students can be encouraged to add to their drawings and revise them as they learn new or additional information. Revising sketches as they read or afterward demonstrates deeper comprehension and attention—we want students to continue thinking as they read further. Sketching can also deepen comprehension differently than linear notes, which can be copied verbatim without much thought or synthesis.

Let's try it here. Read through this poem once without a pencil in hand.

I Wandered Lonely as a Cloud

BY WILLIAM WORDSWORTH

I wandered lonely as a cloud
That floats on high o'er vales and hills,
When all at once I saw a crowd,
A host, of golden daffodils;
Beside the lake, beneath the trees,
Fluttering and dancing in the breeze.

Continuous as the stars that shine
And twinkle on the milky way,

They stretched in never-ending line
Along the margin of a bay:
Ten thousand saw I at a glance,
Tossing their heads in sprightly dance.

The waves beside them danced; but they
Out-did the sparkling waves in glee:
A poet could not but be gay,
In such a jocund company:
I gazed—and gazed—but little thought
What wealth the show to me had brought:

For oft, when on my couch I lie
In vacant or in pensive mood,
They flash upon that inward eye
Which is the bliss of solitude;
And then my heart with pleasure fills,
And dances with the daffodils.

Now read through a second time, and just think about how you would sketch the gist of each stanza. Note how your thinking differs. Do you find yourself going back and forth as you synthesize words and phrases? Or are you reading and synthesizing line by line? Which words resonate most? What catches your attention? What do you ignore?

Now grab a pencil and sketch away. Sketch for no more than 1–2 minutes per stanza. Again, note your thinking. How often did you refer back to the text? How much did you pull in your own schema to create your visual? How do your sketches represent your values or experiences? Did you have enough time? How does sketching capture the gist differently than a written analysis? Additionally, what was your thinking about the text itself? Can you see how you might be prompted to choose certain texts differently, with a slightly different approach to comprehension objectives?

As you can "see," this interaction with the text is constant, detail-oriented, and more intense than skimming through with a normal read. Three simple steps are all it takes. And yes, a little more time to reflect.

1. Read.
2. Read and think about words that create your mental imagery (circle, underline, or highlight them).
3. Sketch away.
4. Share your creativity (optional).

Many of your students will embrace it—my students always want me to sketch when we're reading or learning new content, and it has become one of their favorite routines. I find quick sketches in their margins while they read; even my youngest, struggling third graders love to ask if they can "draw a picture, too" as they respond to questions in writing.

Connections and patterns of their thinking and their knowledge also become more readily available when laid out in front of students. That mental imagery starts to become more organized, which is key for learners struggling with executive functions around organization and attention. Ideas can be delicate and fleeting; crystallizing them and converting them from thought to paper, from mental image to visual image, is crucial for learning.

Listening, synthesizing, then laying it out on paper is your role—and soon, your students' role as visual note-takers. The magic of visual note-taking lies in its ability to distill information to its core, while simultaneously calling into play the most unlikely of details. It's as if a magical window is opened into your students' eyes, and consequently yours as their teacher. You immediately see what's going on inside, often without a word.

Visualization is one of the first reading strategies teachers should model when teaching reading and listening comprehension—and it pays to take it one step further to enhance students' metacognition. No matter the grade level, no matter the language proficiency. Doing so links the words on the page or from the speaker to the pictures in their heads. Goudvais and Harvey report that readers who visualize experience richer reading and retain more details longer.[41] Knowing what we do about the neural machinery of visual perception, we understand how pervasive and powerful visuals are for any kind of learning and comprehension. Visuals in the mind, or mental imagery, draw on much of the same neural machinery but also extend the involvement of other areas in the brain for a holistic learning and memory experience. Share this information with your students.

Remember, however, there can be no memory experience if there is no meaning in the information we pass along to our students or help them learn. What ultimately matters for learning is what we do with that information, what our students are able to do, and the con-

_____

41 Stephanie Harvey and Anne Goudvis, *Strategies That Work: Teaching Comprehension for Understanding and Engagement* (Portland, ME: Stenhouse, 2007).

text through which we each interpret it (or not). Edu-sketching is a learning strategy—a means to access knowledge, synthesize learning, enhance recall, and aid oral and written expression of that knowledge. It is cohesive—"drawing" students together as they share meaning, share nuances, and negotiate complex ideas. Learners literally see their ideas more clearly, as well as meaning—and they can also see what's missing, whether it be pieces of the puzzle or comprehension. It has revolutionized some business boardrooms—why shouldn't it be used with our students?

Aim for students to read, write, listen, speak, and think everyday—and if possible, to edu-sketch.

We need to see things, not just hear them, to learn well. Multisensory and complementary, the verbal and the visual. Take the time to include them both. The mind's eye is a terrible thing to waste.

P.S.

Yes, it sounds simpler than it is. If you're hesitant or in doubt, do me a favor.

Start your thinking with "What if . . . ?"

Just once.

Imagine the possibilities.

Imagine the possibilities for your students' thinking and your own.

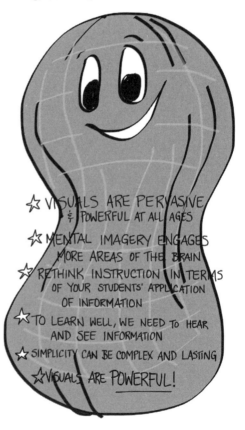

CHAPTER THREE: IN A NUTSHELL

☆ VISUALS ARE PERVASIVE & POWERFUL AT ALL AGES

☆ MENTAL IMAGERY ENGAGES MORE AREAS OF THE BRAIN

☆ RETHINK INSTRUCTION IN TERMS OF YOUR STUDENTS' APPLICATION OF INFORMATION

☆ TO LEARN WELL, WE NEED TO HEAR AND SEE INFORMATION

☆ SIMPLICITY CAN BE COMPLEX AND LASTING

☆ VISUALS ARE POWERFUL!

You Know the Reason Why—Now Let's Get Started

Learn how to see. Realize that everything connects to everything else.

—*Leonardo da Vinci*

And you who wish to represent by words the form of man . . . relinquish that idea. For the more minutely you describe, the more you will confine the mind of the reader. . . . And so it is necessary to draw.

—*Leonardo da Vinci*

If I asked you when you were in kindergarten to raise your hand if you thought you could draw, your hand would fly up without a second thought.

If I asked an entire room full of adults to do the same, I might see one or two hands raise. On a good day.

If you're one of those whose hand didn't move, I'm here to tell you now: Get over it.

This chapter will show you how simple it is to get started with edu-sketching, using just paper and a pencil. I've provided plenty of examples to use in your classroom tomorrow. If you have new ideas, or think you can tweak something to make it work better for you, then by all means, do so. (Once again, you'll see how even the simplest of sketches can inspire new thinking, new perspectives, and aha moments—and if that works for you, imagine your students' reactions.)

Edu-sketching is a strategy that can be used by all teachers and students no matter the content, learning abilities, challenges, or need for more challenges. When determining your sketching tools of choice, be they high-tech or low, simply remember this: Choose and use whatever is the most comfortable for you. Comfort with your tools (a.k.a., magic ink sticks) will equate to successful edu-sketching.

We will start with basic drawing ideas, including shapes, lines, connectors, lettering, and aspects of structure. And please, please, stop. Yes, you. We've already debunked your mental hang-ups about not being able to draw (have you seen my drawings?!), but we'll hit home with that here in this chapter. I will divert, if not transform, your concerns about not being able to draw. Just as with our students, our emphasis needs to remain on the goal of maximizing our thinking processes. Process over pretty (POP)!

In changing the way we—and our students—think, I'm asking you to practice sketching out ideas in the margins and spaces in this book, and to create a personal library of images as you begin seeing things differently yourselves. You will discover plenty of examples. Begin collecting your own compendium of images, according to your context, and start thinking about what might be the most useful or feasible in class. Find a hook, if you will, to your students' and your own internal references. Ideas to keep it fun, fresh, and relevant are included in this chapter, too, to keep your thoughts rolling. Steal what you wish, tweak what you wish, and please, always remember our mantra: POP!

Lest you worry about changing the way you teach or think, remember you already use visual language tools in your classroom, thanks to your huge visual processing propensity. Once you

grant yourself that little nugget of confidence and affirmation, you can focus on the content and the process more deeply. (That's a great note to remember as you start using this with your own students.)

FAVORS I ASK OF YOU

1. Keep a visual record of your growth. Stash any drawings you make as you read this book—personally, I like a sketchbook, so I can look at pages of practice, ugly drawings, and progress. It's all about assessment, right? Create your own pre-assessment and post-assessment; you will be impressed with how far your mind and creativity have traveled.
2. Be patient. Process over pretty. Done is beautiful. Progress one sketch at a time. Build upon your

skills step by step. Changing your thinking and stepping out of your comfort zone isn't the easiest thing to do. You've got this.

3. Risk failure. Cliche, perhaps, but shun complacency. Veer away from your normal zone of reference and send your internal critic packing. Use a pencil if it makes you feel better (that magical eraser),

Even small steps out of our comfort zone can work magic!

and freak out now, so you get it over and done with. What is the worst possible thing that could happen? Everyone freaks out when they're trying to grow—that means you're onto something. Think through all your biggest fears about trying this.

Good riddance!

There. Done. So? What is the worst that could possibly happen? You've already faced it in your mind and dealt with it.

To paraphrase Vincent van Gogh, "If you hear a voice within you say 'you cannot sketch,' then by all means sketch, and that voice will be silenced."

Moving on.

4. Have fun. Enjoy the process. You're going to come up with some silliness, and your sketches will be far from perfect—ride that wave. Your students will embrace the knowledge that it's about the process. And just like usual, they will feed off your energy.

It's about the process . . . it's about the process . . . it's about the process . . .

It's amazing how you can tweak ideas and sketches by the end product when you're enjoying yourself, have ditched your self-critic, and have found yourself in a near-meditative flow state during more intense sketch jams. (And oh, that state of meditative flow. It seems to work with even my busiest, most active students—bonus!)

5. Prepare your materials stash. Okay, seriously. Here's what you need to have in your edu-sketch pocket. Quite simply, something to write and sketch with, and something to write and sketch on. I use markers and pens in my own sketchbook, and markers on a whiteboard or chart paper in class. My students typically use pen-

cil and sometimes go back over their work with colored pencils and markers. Hanks and Belliston like pencils but recommend that folks "begin drawing with a pen. . . . A pencil causes many people to become 'fix-up' artists. You need to be committed— once the pen makes a mark the deed is done."[1] I love that boldness, and I happen to agree—but you need to know your audience. How committed can you encourage your students to be?

In my experience, the younger students preferred to use pencils, too, but I also found that limiting their drawing space made it less daunting and gave them greater courage to dig right in. The bigger the space you give your younger sketchers, the more likely they are to, well, freak out. And while freaking out might be a good sign that you (as an adult choosing to read this book) are stepping out of your comfort zone, it's not such a good idea for our students who need their dopamine surges to keep them engaged and trying. Older sketchers, say, in ninth or tenth grade, can be prone to freak out, too, but they're pretty bold, as adolescents are wont to be. They respond well when you focus on their thinking process and how their sketches actually represent a given concept. Harness their instinctual boldness.

Personally, I like markers with different thicknesses, and love calligraphy markers with varied tips, especially for shaded lines, contrasting thicknesses, and my lettering. I often use black as my basic color because it pops and is the most visible. I also stick to three or four colors per sketch. It seems less overwhelming to me, although I've seen some gorgeous sketchnotes with a rainbow of colors. In the classroom, three or four colors helps me contrast ideas, link others together, and break up any visual monotony without being overwhelming. Again, your preference, but limiting colors in my classes minimizes distraction from the content. Remember that darker colors work best for visibility.

We don't need anyone freaking out. A lack of dopamine doesn't bode well for your thinking capacity. No stress. No freaking out. Pencil with eraser? Yes, sure, fine. Pens? Yes, sure, fine. Colored pencil? Yes, sure, fine. Let's see what you can do!

The five favors I ask of you, again, in a nutshell? For your edusketching journey, bring:

- a visual record,
- patience,
- risk,
- fun, and
- materials.

---

1 Kurt Hanks and Larry Belliston, *Rapid Viz: A New Method for the Rapid Visualization of Ideas* (Boston: Cengage Course Technology PTR, 2006).

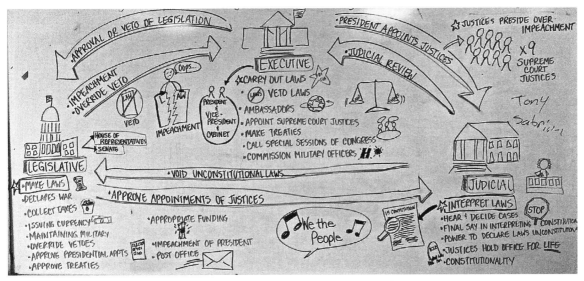

Notes on our classroom whiteboard about the three branches of government.

Notes on our classroom whiteboard about different aspects of plants.

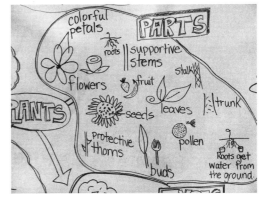

These served as a reference for several days. Even after they were erased, students would still point to the specific areas of the sketch.

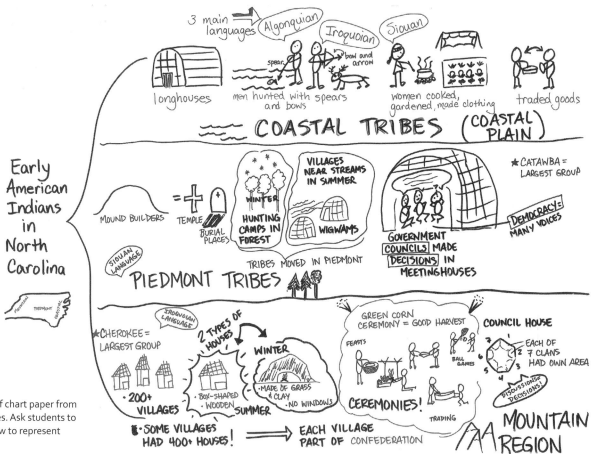

Early American Indians in North Carolina

3 main languages — Algonquian · Iroquoian · Siouan

longhouses

men hunted with spears and bows — spear · bow and arrow

women cooked, gardened, made clothing

traded goods

COASTAL TRIBES (COASTAL PLAIN)

MOUND BUILDERS

TEMPLE · BURIAL PLACES

WINTER — HUNTING CAMPS IN FOREST

VILLAGES NEAR STREAMS IN SUMMER

WIGWAMS

★ CATAWBA = LARGEST GROUP

DEMOCRACY = MANY VOICES

GOVERNMENT COUNCILS MADE DECISIONS IN MEETINGHOUSES

SIOUAN LANGUAGE

TRIBES MOVED IN PIEDMONT

PIEDMONT TRIBES

IROQUOIAN LANGUAGE

★ CHEROKEE = LARGEST GROUP

· 200+ VILLAGES

2 TYPES OF HOUSES

· BOX-SHAPED · WOODEN — SUMMER

WINTER — · MADE OF GRASS & CLAY · NO WINDOWS

★ · SOME VILLAGES HAD 400+ HOUSES! → EACH VILLAGE PART OF CONFEDERATION

GREEN CORN CEREMONY = GOOD HARVEST

FEASTS

BALL GAMES

CEREMONIES!

TRADING

COUNCIL HOUSE — EACH OF 7 CLANS HAD OWN AREA

DISCUSSIONS & DECISIONS!

MOUNTAIN REGION

Notes taken on a piece of chart paper from an article in Social Studies. Ask students to help provide ideas on how to represent main ideas and details.

READY, SET, DRAW

Pencils ready? Markers?

Here's what you can already draw. Draw each of the following basic lines and shapes in five different ways. Kids, by the way, don't seem to need these nudges as much as adults do.

Lines

Squiggle

Zig zag

Straight

Diagonal

Spiral

Shapes

Square

Circle

Rectangle

Triangle

Other shapes

See? That wasn't hard, was it?

Now that you've proven you can draw by drawing these shapes, here's the next step.

Work together with your students to brainstorm what different lines, shapes, and other squiggles could be. When you think you're done, rotate some of the images to see if they spark your imagination even further. Here are some examples from my students, both younger and older.

These are examples of brainstorming with shapes. My high school students love tiny sketching, while elementary students will typically take more space.

Fuel their thinking with a shape warm-up. What can they create from circles that represents an upcoming topic? Or a topic they learned yesterday?

What can you and your students create out of specific shapes?

A fun and challenging application of this activity is to use certain shapes or combinations of shapes to represent a particular topic or theme. How can you represent the Reformation with only triangles? Which combination of three shapes can you use to represent the Louisiana Purchase or types of landforms on earth?

It's worthwhile to remember, too, that creativity is completely subjective. What one person values artistically may not resonate with someone else, and that's perfectly okay. This is process over pretty: we're simply aiming to ramp up some creative juices with this warm-up.

Speaking of shapes, if you can draw the aforementioned basic shapes, you're more than equipped to draw people. I prefer stick figures, including boxy stick figures, in my sketches because they're quick and flexible for nearly any sketching need. Star figures are another favorite because they are super quick to draw.

Letters and Typography

One of the easiest things I've done to promote lettering and typography is to print out the alphabet from Word using 5 to 10 different fonts that I think are replicable. Enlarge and print out lower- and uppercase letters, so that students can play around with different ones. Let students experiment and get comfortable with new types of lettering, or tweaks to their own. (Watch their confidence grow and notice how much lettering shows up on their notebooks and papers.)

What can you come up with? (By the way, it might be a challenge to do this without laughing.) Need an extra challenge? Ask students what they can draw for a given topic using only certain basic shapes. Extend it further by having them use abstract figures or a mix of different geometric shapes. Ask students to represent your given topic using three to five circles or three to five different lines or shapes as starters. You might be pleasantly surprised at their ingenuity.

Encourage students to label what they know. (They may know what they draw, but not the English word. I help if they want, but that's not what this activity is about. It's more of a primer for their imagination, but certainly a bonus if we can attach new words and phrases, too.)

They may "just" be stick figures, but you can still have a lot of fun!

Different fonts can serve as an entryway into sketching for students who may otherwise be reluctant to draw.

TIPS:
☆ NEATNESS MAKES A DIFFERENCE!
☆ FIND A FONT THAT YOU CAN WRITE QUICKLY & LEGIBLY
☆ SAVE "FANCY" LETTERING FOR TITLES & HEADINGS
☆ FOR STUDENTS, FOCUS ON THE CONTENT — LETTERING CAN OFTEN BE A "SAFE ENTRY POINT" INTO SKETCHING, THOUGH, FOR RELUCTANT STUDENTS (SO, KNOW YOUR LEARNERS!)
☆ VARY THE LETTER ALIGNMENT — TRYING TO LINE UP EACH LETTER IN AN EXACT LINE CAN BE FRUSTRATING AND DISTRACTING
☆ PLAY AROUND, EXPERIMENT, ESPECIALLY WITH THICK & THIN MARKERS!
☆ ADD COLOR!

Connectors and Separators

Symbols used to connect ideas or separate them certainly don't need to be fancy. Here are some examples. Try your hand at your own.

Edu-sketching doesn't have to be fancy, but you can see how it helps clarify and chunk information and helps you assess different aspects of comprehension and language. You can provide some of the information and let students fill in the rest, or students can draw as you do, or they can help you come up with ideas for your edu-sketches. The more engaged they are, the better. My high schoolers moaned and groaned a bit when I started this one, but afterward,

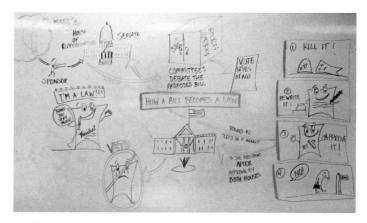

Another example of drawing on the board as we talk through a process. It then serves as a tangible review of the steps.

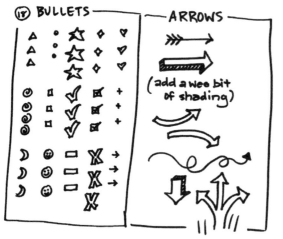

The only kind of bullets allowed in school.

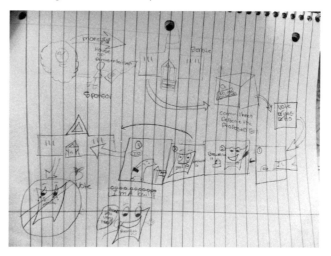

several of them took pictures of the board and claimed they would always remember the process for how a bill becomes a law after crafting this edu-sketch.

Simple graphic organizers can be enhanced with color. Have students go back to their graphic organizer the following day and highlight or outline connected ideas with the same color. Alternatively, use color as you are creating a graphic organizer for another layer of explicit, rapid connection. And as you can see in these examples, process over pretty (POP) definitely rules.

I've purposefully included very simple student-created graphic organizers, some drawn by academically struggling students.

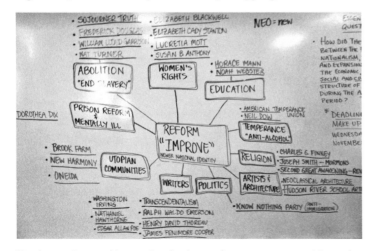

Not the prettiest graphic organizer, but it served as a great metacognitive tool for loaded content review, heavy with multiple key figures. This was done on the whiteboard during class as we discussed each person.

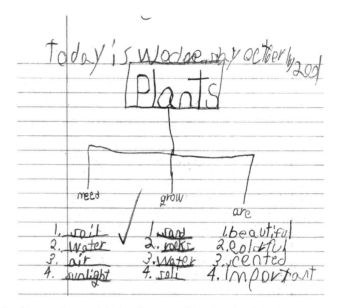

Graphic organizers can't be beat for categorizing thoughts. They're a great starting point for edu-sketchers, for determining relationships among information.

In the figure above there is a simple tree chart, with subject, verbs, and modifiers (direct objects, nouns for prepositional phrases, and adjectives). For this student, the graphic organizer served as a starting point for connecting facts, then writing complete sentences with new vocabulary.

As you can see by the next images, once students get the hang of it, they begin to create their own style—these are chapter-by-

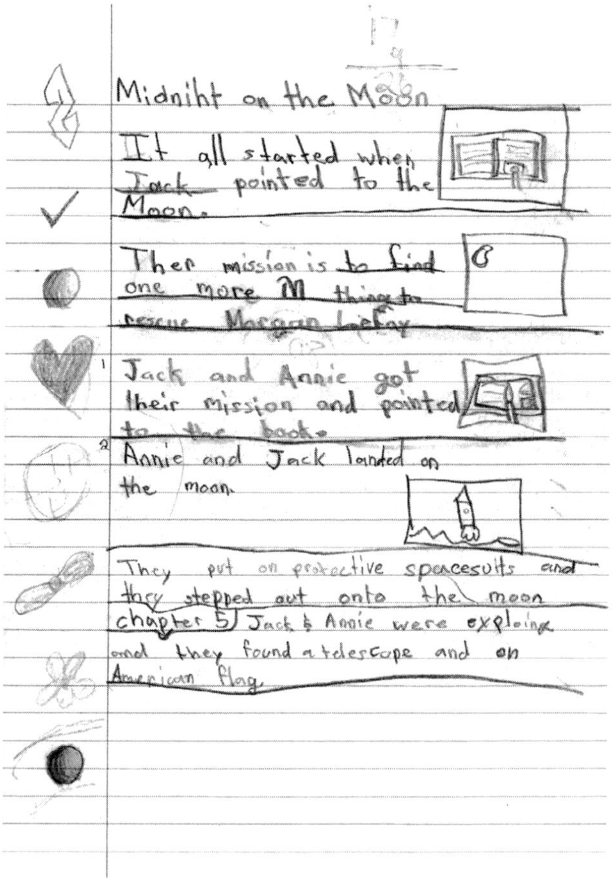

Midniht on the Moon

It all started when Jack pointed to the Moon.

Ther mission is to find one more M thing to rescue Morgan LeFay

Jack and Annie got their mission and pointed to the book.

Annie and Jack landed on the moon.

They put on protective spacesuits and they stepped out onto the moon. chapter 5 Jack & Annie were exploing and they found a telescope and an American flag.

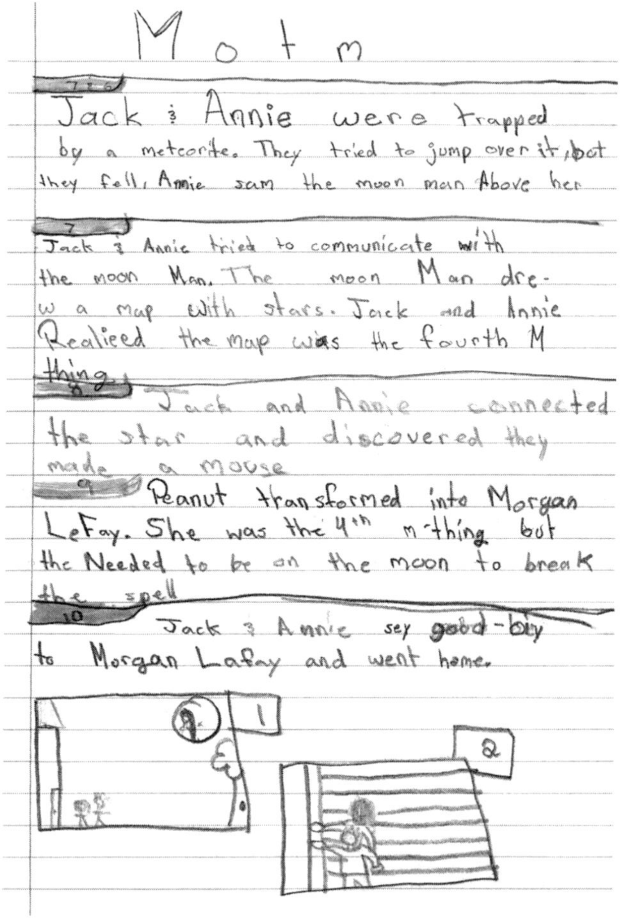

M o t m

Jack & Annie were trapped by a metcorite. They tried to jump over it, but they fell, Annie sam the moon man Above her

Jack & Annie tried to communicate with the moon Man. The moon Man drew a map with stars. Jack and Annie Realized the map was the fourth M thing. Jack and Annie connected the star and discovered they made a mouse

Peanut transformed into Morgan LeFay. She was the 4th m-thing but the Needed to be on the moon to break the spell

Jack & Annie sey good-by to Morgan Lafay and went home.

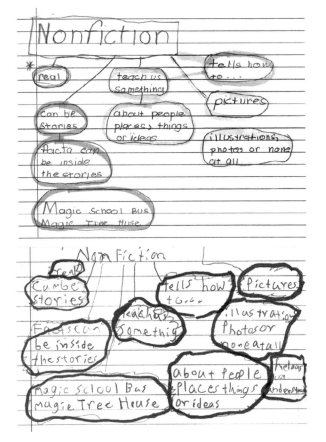

The students used different colors to categorize information making patterns apparent. This is something we did the following day—the day after writing the information—as a review.

chapter summaries of a Magic Tree House book titled *Midnight on the Moon.*

The examples to the left demonstrate simple brainstorming bubble maps, to which students returned the following day with colored markers to review connected information. Below is an example of how students began to include simple sketches on their own within their graphic organizers. On page 96 is a flowchart from a high school student making sense of a dense history text.

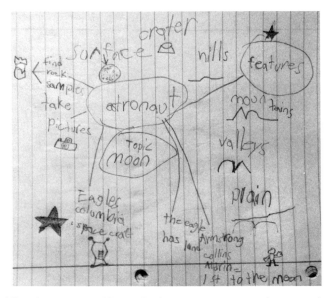

Adding pictures to a graphic organizer is an easy way to get students started.

Students can also use flowcharts to sift through dense texts.

Using bubbles to set information apart also helps to emphasize categories and how information goes together. This is something I am very explicit about as I create notes on the board.

Once students begin to add more information on a page, they can use shapes to set information apart. This still links information within the larger context.

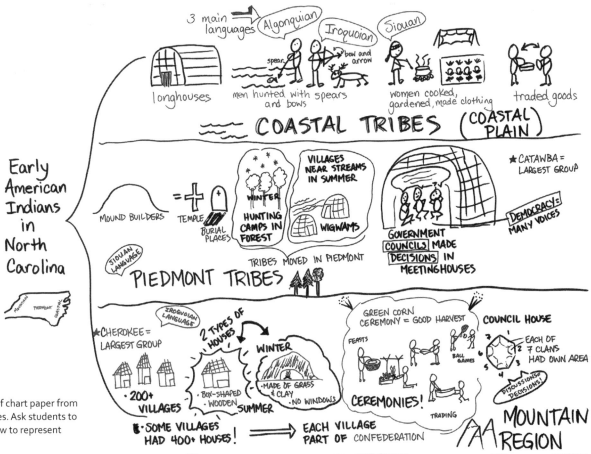

Notes taken on a piece of chart paper from an article in Social Studies. Ask students to help provide ideas on how to represent main ideas and details.

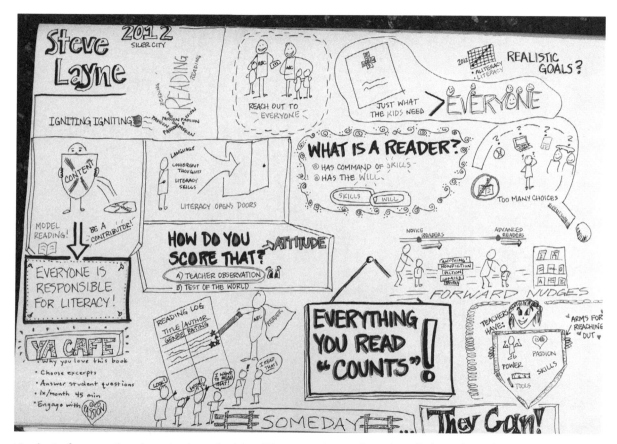

Visual notes from an author who spoke at our school. I used these notes the next day to then talk about what we learned, and discuss some of his ideas. Without these notes both the students and I would have forgotten many of the details.

PATTERN SEEKING

Our brains have an automatic penchant for patterns. For example, certain features of an object, or even a simple line, can trigger recognition in your brain.

Quick—how would you finish these lines?

What would you consider these sketches to be?

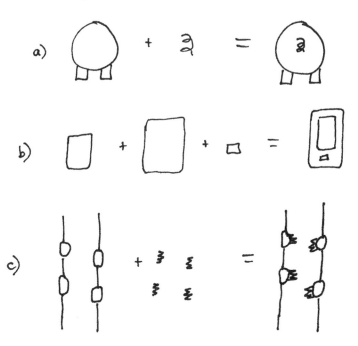

Simple squiggles and shapes, when combined, create something totally new. Kids, of course, know this. We adults seem to have forgotten how much fun it is. Adapted from *The Tell-Tale Brain: A Neuroscientist's Quest for What Makes Us Human* by V.S. Ramachandran. Copyright © 2011 by V.S. Ramachandran. Used by permission of W. W. Norton & Company, Inc. and Penguin Random House UK.

This shows us how even simple features of a sketch can stand in for more complex objects. When you see segments of a visual scene, your brain conducts what researchers call segmentation—determining which pieces fit together to create that whole. This, of course, was a primary survival skill—helping humans detect danger by distinguishing camouflaged animals from the trees. What this means for you, dear edu-sketchers, is that relief is in store; no worries about someone failing to interpret your sketches. Their brains will tend to do so with incredible automaticity, if even only part of your sketch resembles your intended target.

And remember, your brain can only truly pay attention to a single aspect of an image or entity at a time—those overlapping neural networks, as active and efficient as they may be, are in constant competition for your limited attentional resources.[2] Your primary visual cortex, home of your earliest visual processing stages, responds the most to boundaries and edges, not so much to colors and other features. Those singular lines in your sketches—those outlines—are, quite simply, where the action is. In other words, give the humble sketch its cognitive due.

Done. Yep. That's it. Ask any sketchnoter (visit works by Mike Rohde, Sunni Brown, Dan Roam, or Peter Durand, to name a few) and they'll tell you the same. The more you draw, the better you'll get. Take it from Mike Dutton, a professional Google doodler. In a personal interview with him at the Googleplex in Mountain View, California, he repeatedly stated how integral it was to his creative process to make lots of bad sketches. He said that sometimes, in

quest of that perfect sketch, he could create over 400 "bad" ones just to find that quintessential representation—completely understandable given how many people will see his final doodle once it's up and running on the Google home page. The magnitude of his audience also explains his time spent conducting research for given doodles to ensure historical or otherwise factual accuracy. The point is, even professionals don't always get it right the first time. Persistence is key. And patience. And vision. And inspiration.

In my classes, I haven't striven for that level of sketch perfection, nor have I demanded the nitty-grittiest of details, but I do expect students to be able to justify their reasoning behind more abstract sketches—orally or in writing. And that, my friends, is the most

Simple sketches as a warm-up response before reading: What are four images that come to mind when you hear the word "American"?

---

2 V. S. Ramachandran, *The Tell-Tale Brain* (New York: Norton, 2011).

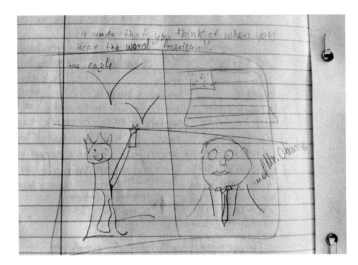

Despite the varied artistic abilities, this quick assessment helped me gain quick insights with laughter and easy conversation.

insight-provoking aspect of doing this in class. Three minutes of sketch time can open vast windows into the worlds of your students' minds, inspire conversations to understand their thinking, and push others' thinking through sharing. We'll talk more about that later.

START EASY

One of the most frequent ways I use sketching is with vocabulary. I may ask students to create a grid, with the word, a sentence or defi-

nition, and a sketch. Don't underestimate the power of your students' minds—I've done that before and have been duly humbled by their knowledge.

Let's try it first. How would you represent the following terms or concepts? Give yourself 1 or 2 minutes per sketch, then turn the page. While you are sketching, be aware of the thinking involved —which experiences come into play, which images you mentally manipulate, and how you ultimately determine your final representation.

Travel

Sigh

Tight

Drama

Thrills

Admire

Here are student examples of these words, which were done either during classtime or as homework, by third graders. These are some of my favorites—their representation of abstract concepts made me smile and nod my head. Never underestimate the power of your students' understanding, no matter where they are in an official proficiency range.

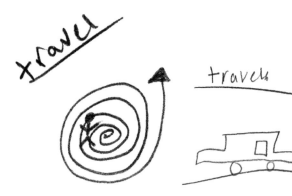

What was your focus for travel?

Even abstract ideas and words can materialize into a sketch.

What heartens me most is when students start to use this strategy on their own. One student gave this sketch to me when we started something new and challenging. This was his way of letting me know he was frustrated. Below is another example.

One night when I asked my second grade son how to encourage my third graders to try harder when they faced challenges, he remained quiet, shrugged his shoulders, then went back to his room. Fifteen minutes later he came out with distilled advice for me to hang in my classroom.

Using words and pictures helps clarify and express thinking that we may not otherwise know about. Pictures are a universal language. Thanks to cave paintings, hieroglyphics, and ancient stone carvings, we know cultures worldwide have used pictures and images as a means of serious communication for thousands of years.

TAKE A CULTURAL LOOK

Yup'ik Eskimo girls pass down their legends and culture by drawing stories in the mud and snow, a fascinating tradition of using symbols to tell a story known as story knifing. They use a decorated story knife carved from hardwood, caribou antlers, or even walrus tusks. Story knives are given to girls (only) as young children, and they, in turn, pass them down to other girls once they hit puberty. Interviews on the American Indian Life Gallery show older women demonstrating story knifing and reminiscing about the hours spent during their childhood days telling stories with their friends.[3] Apparently, it was

---

3 Gretchen McManus, dir., "Storyknifing," American Indian Film Gallery, accessed October 2014, http://aifg.arizona.edu/film/storyknifing.

Used with permission by Diane Suskind

A Yup'ik story knife telling a story

Used with permission by Diane Suskind

Some common storyknifing images. Used with permission by Diane Suskind

common to say to your friends, "Let's go story knifing," and spend hours creating stories in the mud or snow.[4]

4 "Political Archaeology on the Presidents Forum," On the Reading Rest, April 29, 2013, https://floasche.wordpress.com/2013/04/29/political-archaeology -on-the-presidents-forum/; "'Yaaruin' Story Knife," November 4, 2009, http:// yupiitstoryknife.blogspot.com/2009/11/yaaruilta-on-kuskoskwim-river.html; "Story Knife," Alaska Native Collections, Smithsonian Institution, http://alaska .si.edu/record.asp?id=551.

There is also a tradition of "drawing stories" around the world. These are fairly simple tales that are drawn or sketched on a board or large paper by the storyteller while he or she is talking. Listeners watch the drawing unfold, with all of its different symbols, into a single, larger, coherent picture. The combination of listening, watching, and anticipating creates a formula that helps make the story all the more memorable.[5] This can work magic in the classroom—sketching as we go through a story, poem, or other text.

As you incorporate edu-sketching into your classroom instruction, know that there are plenty of ways to make it your own. In this brief chapter, you've seen how easy it can be to draw and create using a minimum number of shapes and lines. Now let's look at ways we can put all of this together.

TELL ME MORE ABOUT HOW EDU-SKETCHING BENEFITS MY STUDENTS

Teachers, you are brain changers. Yes, you. Face it—you have the power to alter students' neural networks, the same ones you learned about in Chapter 2. Sounds daunting, but let me explain.

You see, the more frequently a student's brain retrieves and connects information, the better the chance that the student will recall it quickly and accurately. The memories created through dense, interwoven neural networks are the strongest and most easily accessible (those synaptic connections you learned about in Chapter 2). Information is much more likely to be recalled quickly if it has been retrieved repeatedly and connected to as many other pieces of information as possible.

However (and this was a huge wake-up call for me), even a densely connected, sensory-rich memory is essentially reconstructed when it is recalled. The recalled information can be shaped by context and influenced by the student's emotional state, attention level, and receptivity.[6]

That's a lot of responsibility. As teachers, what are some ways we can create these dense, interwoven networks? How can edu-sketching help students forge long-term memories that will boost their future learning?

5 A. Pellowski, *Drawing Stories from Around the World and a Sampling of European Handkerchief Stories* (Westport, CT: Libraries Unlimited, 2005); R. Thompson, *Frog's Riddle and Other Draw-and-Tell Stories* (Buffalo, NY: Annick, 1990).

6 W. Pillars, "What Neuroscience Tells Us About Deepening Learning," *Education Week*, Teacher Edition, March 27, 2012, http://www.edweek.org/tm/articles/2012/03/27/tln_pillars_neuroscience.html.

CHAPTER FOUR: IN A NUTSHELL

On the Path to Seeing and Understanding Differently

To turn caring into action, we need to see a problem, see a solution, and see the impact. But complexity blocks all three steps.

—*Bill Gates, Harvard commencement speech*

RETURN TO INFORMATION OVER TIME

Strengthening long-term memory is not merely a matter of squirreling information away but of returning to it and building upon it. It's a continual process rather than a linear, one-stop experience.

With this in mind, here are some memory-building tips for your classroom:

- Plan for pointed repetition and the spiraling of information spread out over time, particularly with complex topics, language learners, and struggling learners. Sketches are an ideal palette to revisit and add details or retell throughout a unit or text.
- Plan weeks in advance, if possible, in order to be more strategic about review and transitions. Think about ways students can represent their comprehension with a quick sketch, vocabulary, or key ideas.
- Ask fewer spontaneous questions, opt for higher-level questioning, and try to create or find opportunities to make connections from the start. Consider whether you want students to create quick sketches or more detailed, concrete, or abstract drawings, as with a "what if" question or prediction.

Sketching at certain points in the reading, during a talk, after a video clip, or while listening to a podcast all help students make their own relevant connections. Sketching promotes rereading, revisiting information, and even oral presentation skills, because the kids enjoy sharing their sketches and explaining them to the rest of the class. Displaying them in a gallery setting in your room throughout the unit, book, or week further promotes review and pride in their work. All of these low-key ideas help students interact with the academic content multiple times and view the same information presented through different lenses (a great life lesson as well).

A key bit of advice, though, is to plan out your stopping points for edu-sketching in class—I call them SASSy points (stop and synthesize). Just as you plan certain questions to ask, certain places to stop when reading, or places for emphasis, think of good points for sketching a synthesis or representation. Sometimes there are obvious spots, but it may be intriguing to test their mental mettle a bit with more abstract concepts, just to get their wheels churning.

An example from my newcomer English language learners was a formative assessment based on a social studies text we had read.[1] They had navigated a text (well above their English proficiency) on Christopher Columbus using various reading strategies, and although they had successfully used their strategies with the

---

1 Newcomers are students classified at Level 1 (6 being the highest) in reading, writing, listening, and speaking according to the language proficiency test.

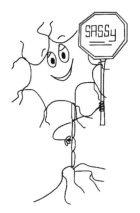

Mnemosyne loves learning!

last half of the text in pairs, then individually, I wanted to make sure they truly understood the text.

I did so through edu-sketching.

Students reread paragraphs I had typed up with important details from the text, and for each paragraph I asked them to sketch the main idea. They reread each paragraph to find details and add them to their sketches. They provided evidence from the text by underlining the words that corresponded with each detail they drew. They did lots of rereading because they wanted to find more details, and because they wanted to confirm what they had done was correct. They also demonstrated their understanding of the individual words as well as the context, when sketching the word or phrase, then underlining each detail drawn.

In all, the students were rereading the text and information at least five or six times on their own, in addition to the original passage they had scoured. And the bonus? They enjoyed the sketching—they compared drawings, laughed, and tweaked theirs after looking at each other's. Little did they realize they were encouraging the repetitive synthesis of information that the relationship-seeking brain craves.

SLOW DOWN

Sometimes we need time to process the glut of information we are presented with. Edu-sketching, even in 2- to 3-minute bursts every 15 to 20 minutes, helps immensely with that synthesis, and with students making connections as they go, not merely at the end. Doing this frequently provides teachers with quick and effective formative assessments as you walk around and engage students in conversation about their sketches or just look. This gives you the timely chance to address misconceptions and misunderstandings.

Another positive aspect of letting kids sketch for even 1-, 2-, or 3-minute bursts is the opportunity to let their minds quiet a little. When teachers ask students a question, the same responders will often have those "helium hands" that pop right up. Rather than suffer through awkward classroom silence, we teachers often succumb after a measly second or two. Asking kids to sketch for just a minute lets everyone get their thoughts together and gives them the opportunity for efficient, thorough memory reconstruction. This is especially critical for language learners who must translate their reconstructions into English.

We are going to visualize. 👀

Long ago, in 1492, three ships sailed to America. They came from Spain. They sailed across the Atlantic Ocean and they sailed on three ships, the Nina, the Pinta, and the Santa Maria.	
Their leader was Christopher Columbus. Columbus was looking for a shorter route to China and the Indies. He wanted spices and gold.	
Columbus landed on an island near the United States. He named the island San Salvador. When he met the Native Americans, he called them "Indians".	
Columbus returned to Spain. Columbus made four trips to America and he claimed the land for Spain.	
Many Spanish people came after Columbus. They started Spanish colonies in America.	

10/10 ✓   ×4

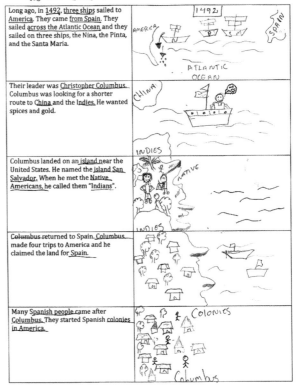

We are going to visualize

Long ago, in 1492, three ships sailed to America. They came from Spain. They sailed across the Atlantic Ocean and they sailed on three ships, the Nina, the Pinta, and the Santa Maria.	
Their leader was Christopher Columbus. Columbus was looking for a shorter route to China and the Indies. He wanted spices and gold.	
Columbus landed on an island near the United States. He named the island San Salvador. When he met the Native Americans, he called them "Indians".	
Columbus returned to Spain. Columbus made four trips to America and he claimed the land for Spain.	
Many Spanish people came after Columbus. They started Spanish colonies in America.	

10/10

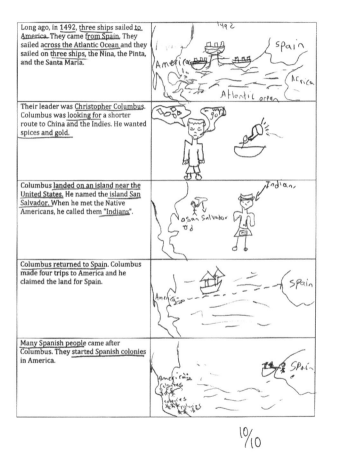

Taking the extra time (truly you can spare a couple of minutes) when you are initiating a topic to have them sketch something they already know helps elicit more than a cursory statement or two. It jump-starts discussions, with the added bonus of helping you tailor your instruction by improving its rigor if they already have a strong knowledge base, or stepping back a bit if they don't. Plus, listening to their peers helps them interlink their knowledge even further, and may remind them of recessed memories.

traditions is Tradiciones	*(sketch)*	The traditions is a holiday.
exports is Exportaciones	*(sketch)*	The EE.UU export many films music.
internet is Internet	*(sketch)*	The internet is very important.
globalization globalización	*(sketch)*	Globalization is a world full of many things

1. Who is your favorite celebrity? Why is that person famous?

my favorite celebrity is Jean carlos ...

2. Do you think the internet is a good thing? Why or why not?

I think the internet is very import... is necessary ...

The second figure on page 110 is an example of a quick draw before we read about celebrities. We drew quick sketches about the concept of being famous, a new English word but not a new concept. Newcomer students sketched what they would be famous for in the future—doing this set the stage for our reading and subsequent discussions, and was an interesting way for them to start our new vocabulary unit. You can see how quickly you can garner snapshots about your students even with the simplest sketches and a short oral explanation.

The figure on the immediate left shows the use of cognates to spur their thinking and how much they already knew prior to reading a more complex text. They could use dictionaries and partners for this activity. Realizing this knowledge prior to reading gave them a needed confidence boost.

TIME IT RIGHT

Here's some cool information. Students tend to be best at recalling the first and last chunks of new information we share with them. Neuroscientists refer to this as the primacy-recency effect. For those of us accustomed to using the beginning of class for review or housekeeping, it seems counterintuitive to think that new information presented first has the best chance of being recalled (due to primacy), while the last information presented has the next best chance of recall (due to recency). Those who study learning cycles also suggest that some sort of consolidation needs to occur about every 20 minutes or so.

So, besides the 2- to 3-minute sketching sessions mentioned above, how else can we use this 20-minute consolidation information in the classroom?

Save the homework discussion, in-depth review, announcements, and attendance for later in the class period. Try to ensure the first 10 minutes are extremely pointed, explicitly linked to the new lesson—a couple of those minutes can be predicting with sketches, or representing a new concept via sketches, as a warm-up. Have students define a new word or two that they will encounter that day, then ask them to represent that concept with a quick sketch. This draws in background knowledge and helps them relate what they know. Sharing out helps broaden those ideas, but you can still guide the discussion through your choice of words.

When reading an article about the migrant wave from the state of Yucatan to San Francisco, our new vocabulary included the word "deport."[2] You can see differences not only in sketch detail, but also perception of the word meaning. Student C has a crying mother, but a smiling father, because he "knows he won't have to worry about going to jail now" in the United States. Another depicts more violent means (guns), while yet another depicts the meaning with boats. You can see what a wonderful jumping-off point quick sketches can be for discussion.

As students learn more about a given topic, they can add to the sketches, a little more each day. Emphasize using an entire sheet of notebook paper, or larger.

---

2 "A Piece of San Francisco Returns to Yucatan with Deportees," *McClatchy-Tribune*, adapted by Newsela staff, May 27, 2014, https://newsela.com/articles/yucatan-sanfrancisco/id/4087/

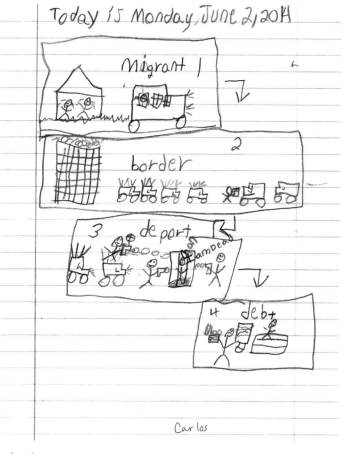

Student A

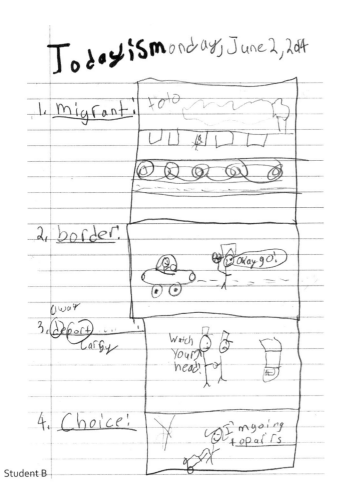

Student B

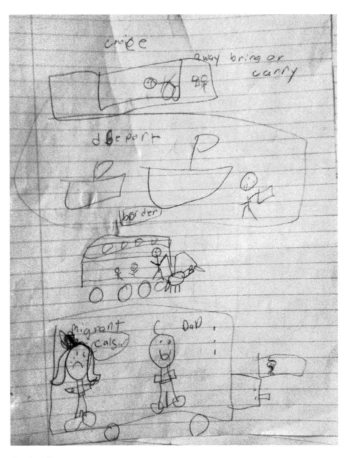

Student C

According to learning cycles, as you now know, about 20 minutes into class it's SASSy time, or stop and synthesize time. Consolidate thinking and improve the chances that knowledge is as connected as possible. (This can be as simple as having students turn to a partner and repeat facts they just learned with a collaborative sketch. If done individually, have them tell a partner one or two details to add to their existing sketch, and vice versa.)

This of course, incorporates speaking, listening, and sketching—with a lovely dash of fun. Keeping a time limit per sketch definitely helps keep everyone on task.

The last 5 or 10 minutes of class constitute the recency period, ripe for another dose of important information. Use that time for closure, asking students for a visual synthesis of information from the lesson, a prediction of what will happen next, or some form of a

"what if" question. If they've already started a sketch, have them add two or three new details to drive home connections, supported by some sort of evidence.

Now, I'm not saying you should do all of this in one class period, every day. What I'm suggesting is that using this as a strategy once in awhile in one of these ways can really improve your students' comprehension of the material they're working with and your vision of their understanding. On the other hand, if your objective is to have them practice the skill of visualizing, then it could be one heck of a fun day with visuals galore. Embrace the change of pace.

Just remember, predetermined stopping points will help things run much smoother.

DEVELOP STRONG RELATIONSHIPS WITH STUDENTS

As mentioned above, memories are retrieved and reconstructed within one's current context. Research suggests that a student's recall of knowledge is determined in part by his or her current emotional state, learning level, attention, receptivity, and other factors.

Attending to the emotional states of our students can no longer be dismissed as too touchy-feely to consider—even by those of us who are self-professed tough-love advocates. The better we know our students, the more we can gauge behavior, beliefs, and feelings that can affect their ability to learn.

Here's something else to think about. Short-term stress hormones like adrenaline have shown positive effects on long-term semantic memory—the memory of what things mean. But a student who is experiencing prolonged stress may have higher levels of cortisol, a hormone that can suppress long-term memory. Not having to worry about getting an exact answer or finding the words to express your thinking are some of the ways sketching can release feel-good hormones like dopamine and oxytocin. Sketching promotes a sense of much-needed calm and time for reflection, while it minimizes stress. Dopamine is also linked to pleasure and, in turn, attention.

Add a little sketch time so your students are at least a little more relaxed, reflective, and attentive.

Recognizing when our students are under stress lets us provide appropriate scaffolding so they can experience some level of success even when challenged. For example, making sure the lesson includes some sort of novelty, such as a prediction or a "what if?" type of sketch, tweaks information that taps into imagination and prior knowledge.

Prompting laughter is far more natural with edu-sketching, too—even 2 or 3 minutes can be meditative and relaxing. If kids are stuck, I like to model an exaggerated sketch, just to ease their minds. This laughter is what suppresses cortisol. Use these opportunities to model a mind-set that helps students control their own stress and anxiety about perfection. By prizing POP (process over pretty), the development of ability rather than perfection of results, that cortisol will plummet.

One obvious way to foster these relationships is to integrate sketching into your instruction and engage with your students one on one. But how do you do that when you have a class of 30 students and a ton of content to get through? Time is tight, and the test looms large, right?

Edu-sketching is only one strategy, but wow, is it a grand one. It can provide invaluable, if unexpected, little insights into your students' noggins. A

Oh, those test pressures!

quick tour around the room will speak volumes and enrich your relationships exponentially. Take the time to ask them about their sketches and why they've included particular details or left others out. Praise the representations and connections they've made rather than artistic ability. Connect students with each other via their sketches: "Hey, you portrayed this nearly the same way as [student]. You should check out that sketch!" or "If you're stuck, take a look at [student]'s sketch, or talk to [student], who has good ideas." You'll discover what resonates with them and why, while performing a covert gap analysis[3]: What does this student understand (or not) that would cause that kind of response? You may discover that more modeling, explanation, or intervention is needed, but little time has been lost—better to discover misunderstanding after 10 or 15 minutes of material presentation than on a unit test.

Don't worry about conversations being awkward. Since the focus is on the sketch, students are far more likely to open up. It's like having those tough conversations with your teenager in the car—not facing each other tends to ease anxiety and nervousness and help open lines of communication.

ESTABLISH RELEVANCE

And of course, the better our relationships with our students, the more effectively we can gauge their prior knowledge and what they

---

3 A gap analysis is the gap between what they should understand/know, and where their actual understanding lies.

truly understand. Help students relate to new information—helping them synthesize the old and the new, we can discover their powerfully established neuronal networks, then "hitchhike" on these networks as we navigate the curriculum.

James Zull states it succinctly in *The Art of Changing the Brain*: "Prior knowledge is the beginning of new knowledge. It is always where learners start."[4] Yet it is frequently a neglected piece of instruction.

One of the most fascinating aspects of edu-sketching is how students will unearth those connections that might otherwise remain dormant. Sketching allows unexpected connections to become visible, and it's exciting. Maybe your language learners (particularly the newcomers) demonstrate that indeed they do have the background knowledge for a particular topic. Without the nonverbal edu-sketching to express themselves, you might never have known because they wouldn't have said anything in class.

In other words, teachers may be brain changers, but we must also give credence to the physical connections our students have already established! Too often, in the interest of expediency, I have assumed what students knew, then proceeded with my planning, my instruction, my connections, on my clock—when it should be about students' learning. In the past I have struggled with frustration at what my students don't get or don't know, when I should be celebrating what they do know and building upon that.

Edu-sketching can do that in spades. As if by magic, students' inner thoughts come out, even if initially hesitant to try drawing

because "it's for little kids" or they "don't know how to draw." You are the one, dear educators, who can make this work—and I can assure you that you will be pleasantly surprised at how students can create more and more connections. Edu-sketching has been a consistent vehicle for the primary reason we learn: to change the learner from a receiver to a producer of knowledge.

Slowing down (as mentioned above) is the cornerstone for much of this. Rather than dismissing or glossing over seemingly random student comments or "incorrect" responses, give students time to explain, especially by referring to their sketches. Using that opportunity to better influence how learning is bridged increases the chances it will be forged in long-term memory.

Relationships, and the strategic investment of time, come easily with these little sketched windows into our students' minds, along with the time to foster personal connections with ease. In the words of Steven Levy, teachers "need to look for the best, expect the best, find something in each child that we can truly treasure."[5]

The tips I've outlined here may

Edu-sketching reminds us to see the gifts in our students.

4 James Zull, *The Art of Changing the Brain* (Sterling, VA: Stylus, 2002), 93.

5 D. Sousa, and C. Tomlinson, *Differentiation and the Brain: How Neuroscience Supports the Learner-Friendly Classroom.* (Bloomington, IN: Solution Tree Press, 2011), 17.

seem obvious—indeed, effective teachers already practice them on a consistent basis. The reasons for edu-sketching are prominent, and the neuroscientific perspective can help us understand exactly why these elements are worthy of consistent implementation: to improve not only the recall of information but students' deeper understanding of our world. And what better way to accomplish this than through connections at all levels?

We've looked at some tips for deepening learning and how they can easily be addressed through edu-sketching. Now let's look at how it can be used within the four different domains of listening, reading, writing, and speaking. (Yes, there is overlap among the domains. Just trying to pass along some ideas here.)

LISTENING

Ironically, one of the least explicitly taught skills in school is listening, yet it's one of the most critical real-life skills—to really listen. Julian Treasure says we retain about 25% of what we hear, even though we spend more than half of our time listening.[6] That's a shame because listening is a tremendous path to much of our understanding, especially for our students who are listening all day in schools.

Edu-sketching is one of the most powerful tools I have ever used to comprehend a talk, lecture, or lesson in real time. Even when I

___

6 Five-time TED.com speaker, author, and sound expert. J. Treasure (2011). *5 Ways to Listen Better*. http://www.ted.com/talks/julian_treasure_5_ways_to_listen_better?language=en

used to be an avid note-taker (I was that go-to person for my notes—not bragging here, but I loved taking notes in high school and college—and shockingly, there was nary a stray line or doodle or sketch in any of them) my brain didn't feel half as tired as it does when I create visual notes now. It is an intense activity, to listen, to take visual notes, to label and phrase aspects of the notes, and to gauge placement of the drawings—because for me it's a one-shot deal. When the speaker is done talking, I'm done taking visual notes. It's done simultaneously.

With my high school language learners, I like to create sketches to pull together lots of information, as a preview, a review, or a study guide. I also enjoy sketching out scenarios or events as we talk about them. They may not be super detailed, but my hope is that it helps pare down some of the masses of information they encounter. Some have pictures, while others rely on color and a graphic organizer for breaking down information.

It has become much easier for me, but not so for our students. They need practice. And lots of it won't hurt them.

I know my English language learners can feel especially overwhelmed by the amount and speed of language they hear while they are trying to process oral information. Listening to extended discourse in one's native language, let alone a second language, can be exhausting. As teachers, we can help them navigate through the language with a couple of strategies:

- Show them how to concentrate on key linguistic ideas in chunks of information. Maybe ask them to sketch a handful of vocabulary words or grammatical phrases that are critical to understanding

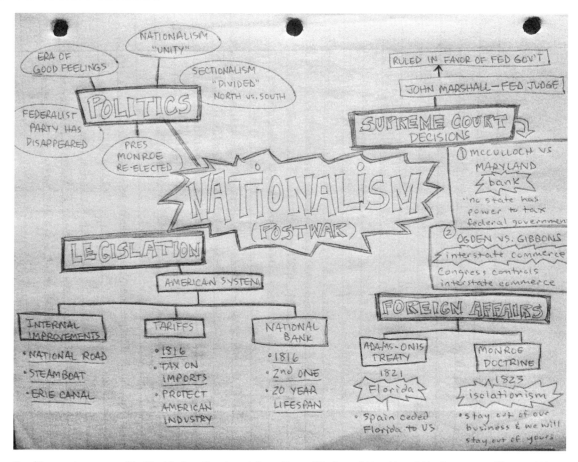

Graphic organizers are a critical tool for breaking down information and finding relationships within the masses of facts and ideas.

the text in advance of the actual listening task. When starting out, consider providing a skeletal outline. The familiarity with the words, even if brief, will trigger their memories, plus they'll already have ready-made images.

- Clarify your objectives and refer back to them during instruction (main idea, vocabulary focus, details, comparing and contrasting, summarizing, predicting). Identify the purpose and expected task or outcome. Should they create a flowchart? A cycle? An image for every 5 minutes? Will these be quick sketches, or will they have time for more detail? Again, consider referring them to specific graphic organizers or flowcharts to contain certain key ideas.
- Once the topic is introduced, elicit key vocabulary from them, rather than giving everything to them first. You can also add more key vocabulary after the listening task. With the vocabulary words, elicit possible representations for even the most abstract words to get their minds in gear. Consider pairing students to spur low-pressure academic discussion.
- Narrow the focus to help students filter details or keep it broad so that students can take it in multiple directions. Make objectives explicit—you may want them to play with several representations before coming up with a single final one to share. On the other hand, you may consider giving them a starting point and letting them fill in details.
- Be open and aware of when their knowledge is activated and they want to take a different direction.
- Create expectations for the listeners. Although it seems basic and so obvious, listening is a very tough skill. Incorporate clear objectives from the start, and start with 3-, 4-, or 5-minute talks before

building up. Five minutes of sustained, intentional listening in order to capture the gist and some details is a challenge!

This is critical for our instruction. Too often, 90 minutes of lecturing are still happening. Without brain breaks to absorb, reflect, and connect, that information will be lost. Even if you're in a hurry, it's better to slow things down than to go fast. Even if students are used to another note-taking format, such as Cornell notes, challenge them to use a certain number of sketches within that format.

Insert an element of competitive rivalry if you must—volunteers can take their place at the whiteboard or with sheets of paper at their seats. Read a selection or part of a selection—or have another student read—while the volunteers sketch simultaneously. See who captured the most key points from the reading. Other students can watch or provide an element of teamwork by reminding the edu-sketchers to add more information or suggest ways of drawing it.

Another key skill set for students is to learn what to do if they can't understand everything they hear.

- Have them work with a partner or small group after the listening task so they can compare notes and clarify information.
- Have successful note-takers and sketchers share their strategies for taking notes and capturing the essence.
- Get students used to listening for the gist and have them represent it via sketching.
- Use repeated listening to focus on adding details.
- Encourage multiple listenings. The more intensive the listening task, the more times they need to listen. As with most things, their

abilities will improve with practice, but the practice needs to be intentional.

- Give them time to modify or confirm what they already have on their papers, and have confidence that your students can independently or collectively create meaning. Use the repetition to add new details with a different color marker or highlighter. Practice, practice, practice!
- Conduct a whole-group after-action review—what worked? What suggestions do they have to make it better the next time? Sharing results with partners, small groups, or the whole class will expand comprehension even further.

Done regularly, listening proficiency will increase, but again, this is something new for many of our students, particularly those who are language learners. Be patient.

After the listening task, make sure to debrief and use the knowledge gained in pointed practice. Ask students to refer directly to their sketches and encourage them to try using both new content vocabulary and familiar words to label and explain their representations. Always make sure you talk about why the task was conducted and what they learned (or didn't) from it. Metacognition, thinking about what works for their own thinking, is such an important aspect of the lifelong learner.

With practice, of course, students will extend their listening skills and rely less on our specific guidance, capturing more ideas that resonate and help them remember.

Active listening, evaluating information in social and academic conversations, distinguishing key words and phrases, differentiating supporting details from main ideas, listening for metaphors, and following oral directions are all benefits of practice in heightened listening.

SPEAKING

As mentioned above, speaking skills can be practiced quite easily with edu-sketching. The most obvious way is for students to navigate, clarify, and share their sketch information with others.

Students can create more formal presentations to explain their sketches, no matter how simple. Insert sketches into a tech-based platform (Keynote, Prezi, etc.) or simply have students present them on paper in front of a partner, small group, or class. Presentations are especially fun for the kids when done with a partner—doubly so if they've sketched together.

Presentations, although seemingly simple, can incorporate multiple speaking skills for everyone. Have students in the audience ask yes-or-no questions, wh- questions—those that require detailed responses beyond yes/no—or find elements of each other's sketches to compare and contrast. Encourage specific vocabulary, maybe a sequence of events or a cycle, or descriptions of people, places, or actions in the sketch. Again, pull in metacognition—"How did you know that?" or "What made you think of that symbol or image?" Support students as they defend and rationalize their thinking with evidence.

But here's the thing. Although seemingly simple, whenever we focus on students' oral language development, it improves their reading ability, both fluency and comprehension. When their reading ability improves, so does their writing. The ones having focused conversations in class, whether persuading, arguing, informing, questioning, or narrating, are the ones who are thinking. And the ones who are thinking? Well, yeah. They're the ones doing the learning.

If we as teachers are always talking, or are talking the majority of the time, who is the one who "knows her stuff"?

Some kids will need linguistic support, no matter their native language. This is academic language, so another nonverbal support can be charts in the classroom—with sketches and pictures. It doesn't have to be fancy, but displaying sentence frames, word walls, and target vocabulary provides solid support. And when the student talk is focused on sketches, it is far less likely to be distracted. A focal point is golden for productive student talk.

Never discount simplicity. Sometimes the simplest sketch comes from a wealth of background knowledge begging for an outlet. Have kids convey their knowledge, convey an experience, or even try to persuade others to view their sketches as they intended (some of the sketches are quick draws, without much detail—these are ideal vehicles for more oral explanation). Have students promote an argument, using the drawings to expand details. Sketches become handy tools to promote speaking and recall specifics.

(Please quit thinking about all the reasons why these ideas wouldn't work in your classroom. You'll never know until you try.) Think "what if . . . ?"

READING

Edu-sketch during pre-reading (predicting), and during reading, post-reading, and re-reading. Create visuals for sentence-level descriptions with explicit vocabulary. Draw a prediction before reading, then another after reading, and have students explain orally or in writing why they changed their drawing. What new knowledge did they gain? What details became important? Create a graph or other table to represent information. Challenge them to sketch ideas or details from one particular point of view; better yet, have them partner with someone sketching the opposing view to fan the flames of discussion.

Sketch the gist of each paragraph in the margin (in a shorter text; smaller space means quicker sketches). Sketch the main idea. Then sketch one or two details, or even the meaning of a particular vocabulary word from each paragraph that you deem central to its meaning. Sketch three symbols to represent the time period, or sketch what you think happened before paragraph one. The ideas are endless, and again, quick is key, as is process over pretty.

Sketching as students go is a solid and effective strategy. They can sketch either near each paragraph or in their notebooks, or you can give them a number of sticky notes. Provide specific SASSy point page numbers (or other differentiated guidance) for them to stop and synthesize if they're doing group or independent work. Afterward, they can sequence the notes as a review.

Note: In my experience, providing time boundaries (2–3 minutes is my default time) or specific numbers helps kids focus on the task at hand rather than aspects of drawing. You can see in the examples that some kids will feel more comfortable with just sketches, while others will want to add words or short sentences. Either is fine—just make sure their outcome aligns with your objectives.

Sometimes you'll want to try something a bit more "sparkly." For example, when we read *The One and Only Ivan*, a story with a gorilla

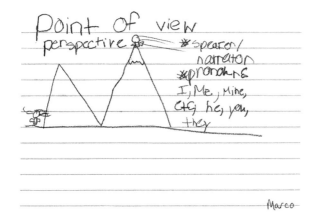

named Ivan as the main character, I brought in a how-to-draw book. We spent about 10 minutes learning how to draw a gorilla step by step, and they loved it. It was a huge motivational factor for them to draw even more detail, plus it encouraged them to seek other how-to-draw books in our school library, then create their own additional comics.

REREADING

One of the toughest challenges my colleagues and I have is getting kids to reread. Assigning them different "missions" to accomplish can encourage them to reread, but not always. Although challeng-

ing, it's important: typical readers simply can't retain what they read after a single go-round (and that would include me, with my distractible brain). We need to reread to keep facts and tidbits in our memory, to keep our brains happy and dendrites nourished to reach out. Edu-sketching is one strategy that works in getting kids to grapple with the text yet again, from different perspectives, and in order to make explicit connections.

Encourage rereading by slowing down to honestly think about the text. Then have students turn to a partner after they sketch the

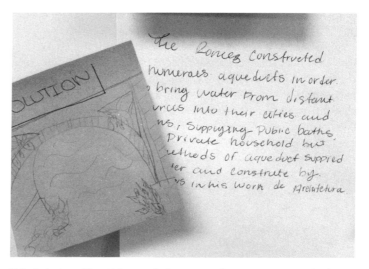

This student used her sticky note for imagery, and wrote sentences on her larger paper. Readers could lift the sticky note to read the sentence underneath.

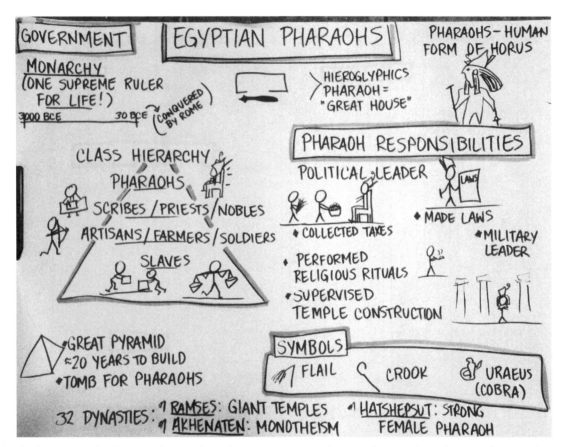

This is an example of a sketch I created in class as we began to learn about Ancient Egypt. It then served as part of our reference wall, and students could use it to guide their own notes.

The limited space of sticky notes tends to make a task more achievable for students than if they used a larger piece of paper.

main ideas of a given part of the text. A quick question to a shoulder partner,[7] such as, "Why did you draw that detail?" or "What does that represent?" promotes accountability and clarifies their thinking. "Where did you find a clue for that detail?" Another idea might be to choose a single word from the paragraph or page that embod-

_____

7 The person next to you—it's a quick method of assessment, reflection, etc., and signals students to ask someone close to you rather then get up and circulate to find someone else.

ies the essence of a chunk of text and sketch it in the margins. Or provide students with part of the text, and at the end of their reading, they can sketch a prediction of what will happen next, or the conclusion. Once you give them the remainder of the text, have them go back to their sketch and make any necessary changes. This gets them to rethink and even justify what they had drawn; as you ask them about their changes, or clues that led them to draw something in particular, they will return to the original text for specific evidence.

Although sketching notes while reading can extend reading time, the benefits are many:

1. Students can return to their notes and add details.
2. Students can synthesize the main idea with words and images.
3. Students can focus on what helps them remember and process information.
4. The sketched notes are easier to retain and make a great review tool.
5. They are a lot more fun to share and revisit.

I find that edu-sketching while reading takes me longer, but it also depends on my audience. If I'm doing it for myself, just to practice creating visuals and to help me understand the text, I will feel more free to play around with lines and imagery, and I think about what resonates personally. If my sketch will be used as a class study tool, or for an otherwise external audience, I want to make sure I include key details that will help them comprehend my sketches in light of the content.

Here is an example of how I synthesized myriad written biographies of a cohort of teacher leaders I was leading. We were discussing our individual types of leadership in an asynchronous thread online, which is the epitome of a linear conversation. It can be really hard to follow or remember details after so many people post. So I plotted folks on the leadership compass as shown here.

You can see how simple it is to make connections, see groups at a glance, and grab a mental image quickly. And it honored the participants, especially since it was done at the very beginning of our cohort. In that sense it helped to provide cohesion from the outset, as well as a ready reference point throughout the months ahead. As it wasn't expected, people were pleasantly surprised.

In general, I aim for expedience and clarity in my sketches. I may or may not create a draft, particularly when it's done on the fly during class. There are times when I practice different ways of sketching

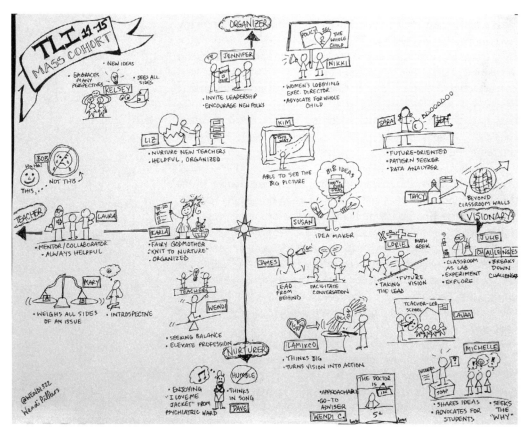

Collection and plotting of teacher leader intros on a leadership compass. This helped us grasp quickly who and where everyone fell in the Native American leadership compass—it was far more expedient and reference-worthy than the multipage asynchronous discussion thread.

ideas when I know I will be sketching in front of the class, or for my own clarification when sifting through dense notes and many facts. This, above all, provides me with the best opportunities for thinking aloud—why I drew this detail and not that, or wondering out loud how activities or objects connect. Kids will jump in and maintain that internal dialogue for their turn at edu-sketching. I know this for a fact, since I overhear students asking each other, "How do these connect?" "Which detail do you think is most important?" "How did you represent this idea?"

As readers, we analyze the main idea, details, and other nuances of a text to absorb the full meaning. When we analyze images, we do the same thing. Some may call it visual literacy, that ability to interpret, recognize, appreciate, and understand information presented through visible actions, objects, and symbols, natural or man-made. In other words, we all rely on imagery—whether literal or symbolic—to navigate meaning in the 21st century. Just think of your cell phone and all of its apps. Instantly recognizable images abound—the Twitter bird, the Facebook "f," or the Google Drive symbol, to name a few—not to mention the ubiquitous icons and symbols mentioned in Chapter 3.

When students are learning vocabulary for the first time, or relearning it within a new context, a little edu-sketching can go a long way. Here are examples of vocabulary sketches drawn after we briefly discussed the definitions. You can see how easy this makes it to assess prior knowledge, while lending insight into the strength and depth of your students' thinking in a given topic area.

Simple assessments can occur quickly—even though one student spelled "learn" as "lean," the sketch shows comprehension of the

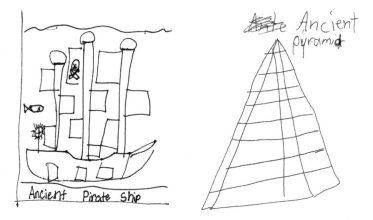

Never discount background knowledge and personal interests!

Again, what's in the minds of our students can't always be determined through words alone. I never would have imagined this is what my students thought was amazing without these quick vocabulary sketches!

meaning of "learn," whereas another wrote "lean" and sketched the meaning of "lean" instead of "learn." In other words, I could see immediately whether it was a spelling or semantic error. Both were easy fixes, with the sketches.

On page 129 you can see I wrote out the words in advance, and assigned one to each student. They, in turn, were expected to create an image based on its usage within context in the novel or document we were reading and explain it to the class. It then served as part of our word wall for subsequent reference.

I can see at a glance that "lean," rather than "learn" is simply misspelled—that she understood the meaning of the word.

©2012 Corinna Gandara

"Lean" in this picture, however, shows me this student misunderstood the intended vocabulary word "learn." He did, however, depict an accurate understanding of the meaning of "lean." The sketches provided quick formative assessments that focused my areas of review.

The words remain visible throughout the unit, and are then hung around the room for the semester for continued reference. (high school, ESL)

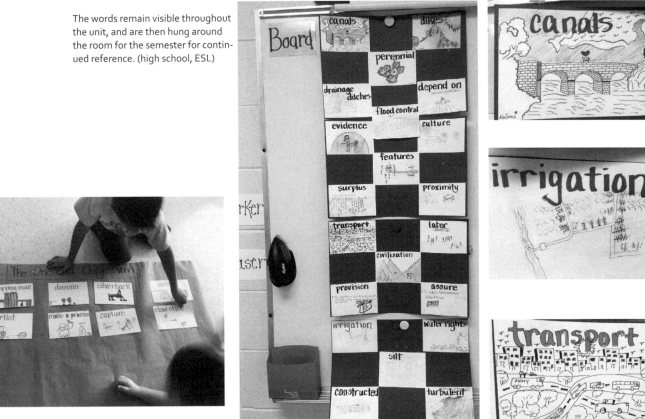

Students use sketches to represent the meanings of vocabulary words for our novel. (3rd grade)

Another way, as we've seen earlier, to assess student understanding is to use multiple vocabulary words and concepts within a sentence, then leave space for students to illustrate them, making sure to represent each of the details. It may seem simple, but done right, it can be cognitively demanding.

Draw a picture for each of these sentences:

1. There is a large crowd at the nighttime stadium.

2. They are celebrating Veterans Day with national symbols.

I wrote sentences with multiple new vocabulary words for an ESL beginner class, and their visual notes showed me their comprehension of each detail in the sentences.

Draw a picture for each of these sentences:

1. There is a large crowd at the nighttime stadium.

2. They are celebrating Veterans Day with national symbols.

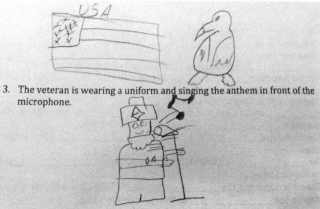

3. The veteran is wearing a uniform and singing the anthem in front of the microphone.

Please respond to the question:
Why is it important to honor and celebrate veterans on Veterans Day?

What edu-sketching does is take it a step further, by having students generate their own visuals. If analyzing images and assessing their point of view or purpose constitutes desired critical thinking, imagine the value of students generating their own images. Having them share their work with partners or small groups ups the academic ante, since you really need to know your content if you want to explain and rationalize it to someone else. There's a lot more thinking going on.

IDEA CATCHERS

Another way to keep track of ideas is to use sticky notes (the Navajo have dream catchers; edu-sketchers can have "idea catchers") or index cards, and that way you can manipulate them on a larger piece of paper later (sequence, compare and contrast with others' responses). Sometimes I use sticky notes to hold ideas that I'm not sure what to do with—although that's more likely to happen while I'm taking notes during a talk. Regardless, using tools like this helps you remember ideas without stressing about the details.

One of the things that people comment on when I create larger visual notes is how I plan out the spacing. I realized it was hard for me to explain—I just do it. I consider the length of a talk, how big my paper is, and start from the gist as provided in advance. But that's tough to impart to kids, so here are a couple of strategies I've found that work if you want students to draw big rather than in their personal notebooks.

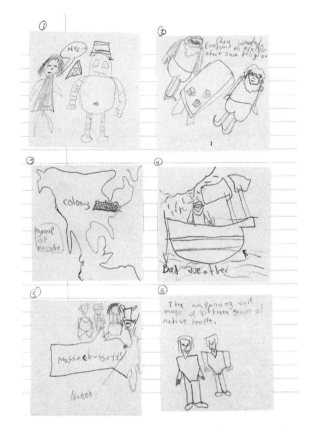

This student's idea catchers chronicle the discontent of the Pilgrims, their journey to their new land, assistance from Indians, and foods at one of their first joint feasts.

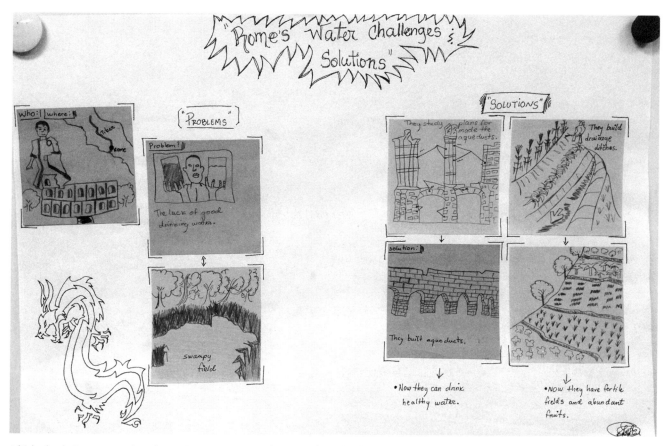

A highschooler's representation of water issues in ancient civilizations. These sketches were created from a challenging document-based unit of study.

Here you can see idea catchers used for a book sequence. The idea catchers were then placed on a sentence strip, and the students were tasked to write questions about the reading at the end of the sequence.

Teachers often ask about how to make the "bigger sketches," and this is an example of a student just trying it on his own, instead of using sticky notes first then redrawing, and instead of folding the paper into sections.

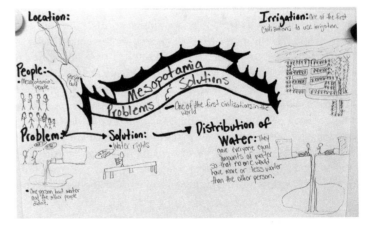

This student used sticky notes first, then transferred his ideas to a larger sheet of paper to summarize a document.

Have students lay out their idea catchers and sort them. For a "closed sort," you provide the categories, so maybe you have beginning, middle, and end. Students would determine which of their cards relate to those categories, then place them on the paper in that order. Maybe there is a single main idea that they can place centrally, then place details around it.

For an "open sort," the kids can come up with ways to categorize and organize their thoughts and sketches. This is an especially powerful activity for teachers to see their students' thinking, and to provide wonderful conversation starters as you walk around the room and monitor their work. Questions such as, "How do those ideas go together? What do those ideas or images have in common?" can be an insightful opener into their world of thinking.

Either way, as kids sort, they are extending their thinking and determining relationships—all while feeding those neural desires to connect. In order to do this, they need to compare and contrast ideas; research shows that strategies that engage students in comparative thinking had the greatest effect on student achievement.[8] As they think about these connections, students have the opportunity to tweak or refine their sketches, which, in turn, lowers their affective filters—which basically means they are encouraged to take risks and shelve their inner critic as they put it all together (the holy grail of teaching there).

And it's tangible. Making thinking tangible, with the sketches and

the manipulation, helps learning come alive for visual and kinesthetic learners. It engages the kids and provokes discussion, not only between you and your kids, but among the students themselves, as they discover new details in each other's sketches, as previously mentioned.

Another strategy for organizing sketches is to ask students to fold their paper into sections, using each section for an individual sketch.

Edu-sketching has the added benefit of promoting community because students are interested in each other's interpretations. It's

---

8 H. Silver, "Section 1: Why Compare and Contrast?" in *Compare and Contrast* (Alexandria, VA: ASCD, 2010), http://www.ascd.org/publications/books/110126 /chapters/Section-1@-Why-Compare-$-Contrast%C2%A2.aspx.

Notes from the novel *The One and Only Ivan* on paper that has been divided into sections by folding.

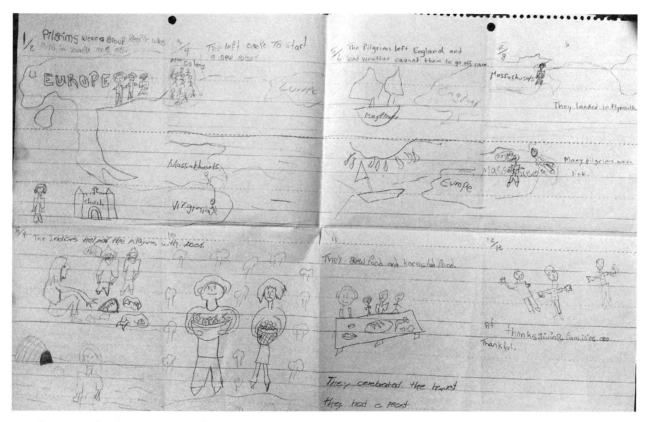

Notes from a text, placed onto larger paper, folded into divided sections to correspond with different points in the text.

relevant listening practice, and they learn to ask questions out of curiosity and a desire to clarify. They're also comparing another's interpretation to their own, thus viewing through an alternate lens on their topic. Once they hear and see others' interpretations, they can have time to add to their own.

Do take the time to teach students about specific levels of questioning, however. Provide sentence starters and question stems from Bloom's taxonomy or a similar questioning hierarchy to prevent questions that are simple offshoots of "What is that?"

WRITING

I'm pretty sure most of you have used imagery in some fashion for writing with your students—maybe as prewriting brainstorming, maybe as illustrations for sections of writing, or a cover image—so this isn't new. When you bring words and pictures together, a little bit of magic happens, and kids instinctively know this. Ideas flow a little more readily when you have a picture in your head. If you put it on paper, though, it gives you time to delve deep into the details before you even start writing. There's a term for that—"transmediation"—when meaning from one system (pictures) is recast to another (writing). Pretty cool stuff. And it supports your students who have little affinity for words, let alone wordsmithing.

How would you represent this thought in writing? Can you picture this as a warm-up for writing, having students sketch the image this poses? What should writing do "in your words"? "The best way to write is to let the image pull you. You should be water-skiing behind it, not dragging it like a barge. Writing should take you for a ride," says writer-cartoonist-teacher Lynda Barry.[9]

Instead of having kids write about themselves at the beginning of the year, have them create a sketch of themselves. Not their bodies, per se, but a sketch with their goals for the year, likes, dislikes, and dreams—whatever you wish. Then they can present the sketches, or students can do a gallery walk with all sketches displayed. There you have the perfect setup for students to learn new things about each other, and compare or contrast, complete "I wonder . . ." statements, and so on, in writing. Much more interesting than a plain old "Hi, I'm so-and-so, and I like such-and-such," especially when the kids have been together for years.

Asking them to picture themselves in positions of success also triggers the visualization effect that athletes and others rely on. Research has shown that visualizing and then sharing your goals can help you make more progress toward them, which is what we did in the figures on pages 134–135. These figures show an autobiographical sketch from a 7-year-old. It's never too early to encourage students to envision themselves each step of the way to their own personal hall of fame.

Warm-up: with my newcomer language learners, we write together at the beginning of class. We start with a greeting and the date, then write a few more sentences, either about the sequence of the learning (with objectives embedded), or about current events. I

---

9 Omega Institute course description for Lynda Barry's "Writing the Unthinkable." http://www.eomega.org/workshops/writing-the-unthinkable-0#-workshop-description-block

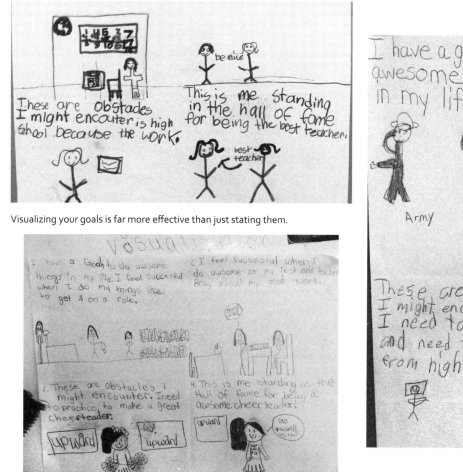

Visualizing your goals is far more effective than just stating them.

These are obstacles I might encounter is high school because the work.

This is me standing in the hall of fame for being the best teacher.

be nice

best teacher

I have a goal to do awesome things in my life.

I feel successful when I get A on my Report card.

Army

These are obstacles I might encounter. I need to be brave and need to graduate from high school.

This is me standing in the Hall of fame for being the best man in the Army!

Visualization

I have a Goal to do awesome things in my life. I feel successful when I do my things like to get A on a role.

2. I feel successful when I do awesome on my test and teacher Brag about my good work.

3. These are obstacles I might encounter. I need to practice to make a great cheerleader.

UPWARD   Go upward

4. This is me standing in the Hull of fame for being a awesome cheerleader!

upward   Go upward! my team

A newcomer with limited native language skills or English language skills can still have goals and express his thinking through sketching.

Spontaneous sketchnote autobiography by a 7-year-old. My all-time favorite!

will often include picture clues with the sentences to provide some anticipatory background for the day's objectives or write something about the students while inserting contextualized vocabulary. This is an easy way to model writing and sketching.

Asking kids to make movies in their mind while they are writing, just as in reading, helps encourage the flow of thinking. Ask them to sketch their favorite part of the book or predict what might happen with a sketch. When they talk about it, it helps with their oral flu-

ency; and if they can say it, chances are good they can then write it more easily. Sketching jump-starts their thinking when it's often so difficult to start writing cold.

Another way we incorporated sketches was by building them into simple feedback and thank-you letters to a classroom guest. She was a Cherokee Indian who brought a plethora of wonderful artifacts for the students to see, touch, and use. It was a natural step for the students to show some of their favorite moments via sketching.

Good morning!
Today is November 14, 2014.

Fredy is sick from his shots. ☹

Rosmery and Selenia are ready to learn.

Ramón is listening to his music.
(but he will stop now!)

Miguel is wearing stripes again today.

English language newcomer daily welcome with sketches and sentences with new vocabulary show how easily (and quickly) we can incorporate sketching to enhance understanding.

Today is November 14, 2014.

Fredy is sick from shots.

Rosmery and Selenia are ready to learn.

Ramón is listening to his music.

Miguel is wearing stripes again today.

SYNTHESIZE AND SUMMARIZE

It's now better known and better understood that when studying or listening for any length of time, it's best to take a break every 15 minutes or so to recap what you've just read or learned. As you know, I call these breaks "stop and synthesize time" (or SASSy time for kicks). Considered "brain breaks" by many or, my favorite, "syn-naps,"[10] these brief 2- to 3-minute working respites can help cement information in our working memory. One way to do this is with a quick sketch with an accompanying sentence about the main idea, or perhaps a vocabulary word that captures the essence of what the teacher just said, what the discussion was about, or a key takeaway from the compare-and-contrast activity they just completed—you name it. Heck, how about a metaphor to illustrate that particular chunk of information? It doesn't even have to be the same for each stopping point. Vary it, and have the kids choose. Ask them to point out appropriate places to stop and summarize, or points where there is important or dense information. Let them do the work. The point is active recall and synthesis of ideas for a quick formative assessment. It not only enhances the memory of our students but also helps us as educators to avoid cruising down the wrong path if half of our students aren't with us. (I know I've said it before, but it bears repeating.)

Here are just a couple of examples from reading. Students were asked to sketch something they learned about ancient Greece and

Despite spelling errors, the comprehension is clear.

10 J. Willis, "What You Should Know About Your Brain," Educational Leadership, ASCD http://www.ascd.org/ASCD/pdf/journals/ed_lead/el200912_willis.pdf

What ancient+I ~~learned~~ about Greece.

Ancient is a synonym for very old.
k very old

What I learned about the Olympics.
I, Jack and Annie go to a Mission.
girl allowed
Jack
The Olympics Rome

What I I learned about Ancient Greece.

I learned about the Olmpics.
That there are more than 20 countrys. Like 88 Country that is

cool

Ancient Greece, with a little modern attitude, but as a formative assessment. I wanted it to be clearer that girls did care about learning.

This student chose to focus on a vocabulary word as one of the things he learned during our text comparisons.

Illustrate two facts that you have learned about Ancient Greece and/or the Olympics. Check out the detail!

about the Olympic games (thereby differentiating fact from fiction in the Magic Tree House book *Hour of the Olympics* and other nonfiction references). Students simply folded their papers in half to respond.

You can see in the third example that I needed to ensure students understood that the girls' attitude toward school was not apathy, and clarify that the Olympics in ancient Greece did not include 88 countries, but that the recent Olympics did. You can also see the difference in focus—Student B focused on a vocabulary word, while Student A focused on girls' participation in school and the Olympic games. Student D included the most detail of any student; art is this student's preferred method of expression.

The examples on the following page show summaries according to different sections of the aforementioned text on immigrants from the Yucatan to San Francisco. Students folded their papers into four sections and sketched the gist of each part. This was then used as a stepping stone for more detailed responses. This was fascinating to me because of the conversations I heard during their sketching. They were talking animatedly about their experience-based knowledge as they sketched, a relaxed, organic discussion far better than anything I could have engineered.

Here, students broke down a complex text into four parts based on the text subheadings, with a main idea from each.

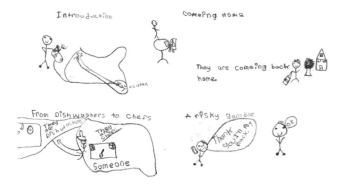

SEQUENCING

Create a flowchart to show the sequence of events in a story. Use boxes to provide limits for your students' writing and sketches, and provide differing clues in each.

In this example, my students practiced using past-tense verbs in each sentence. I drew the first two sketches to show what action was taking place. We discussed the next boxes as a group, and they teamed up to fill in the sentence frames and sketch the meaning. This was a simple review for them.

For my more advanced students, I asked them to complete an entire action, with sentence and sketch, independently. So even a simple activity like this can harness group, pair, and independent work, referencing the text and rereading, using new vocabulary in context and purposeful discussion. It was scaffolded with sentence starters, initial sketches, and modeling. Clues were in the book they had read, and a previous word bank for verbs in the past tense could be used if they needed it.

You can see that it didn't need a lot of set-up time, but students were expected to create their own sequences in their individual notebooks. They filled in their answers first and could change them if needed, which ensured a lower affective filter (not so much stress if they made mistakes), but they were encouraged to try. The pair work engaged them in natural dialogue as they came to the board to write their responses. Students were working on past-tense verbs and vocabulary within the sequential retell.

For reference, I'm including my high school students' notes—notice how tiny their notes are. There is no need to pull out any spe-

Sequenced notes, cloze-style, on the whiteboard in class with students filling in the blanks and edu-sketching.

cial tools, as you can see. This group seems to actually prefer tiny spaces for their sketches.

The next example was another fun challenge for my language

learners. First, they were given the written sections (at the bottom of the page) and tasked to sequence them with a partner. They then sketched what they understood the text to mean. Once they shared with another partner group, they were given the actual illustrations to complete the sequence. This was a self-assessment as well as a comparison of answers. After this step, students wrote one-sentence

summaries to show what they understood. Anytime you throw underwear, let alone "self-cooled" underwear, into the mix, you will grab students' attention.

Notice the variety in student output. This class was a mix of proficiency and ability levels, but they were still able to access information at their own level. Their output professed understanding, and they were able to provide even more detail orally. You can see the literal comprehension in the figure to the left, where astronauts "climb" into their spacesuits via a ladder. This then led to discussion of "climb into" as a phrasal verb, as well as corrections to the sequence.

THINKING

Yep, all of the above. Bits and pieces of knowledge quickly go away. Edu-sketching helps meld those pieces together for a more coherent—thus, memorable—whole.

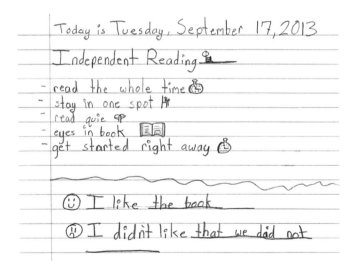

Sketches accompany rules in the classroom, and then in the students' notebooks.

This student used edu-sketching as she read independently and prepared for an assessment of the text.

I know that it works when I see students applying the strategy of edu-sketching on their own, not when asked to do so. It shows that they do benefit from using it, and that they enjoy it. (I may be biased, though—my kids certainly know how excited I get when they edu-sketch.)

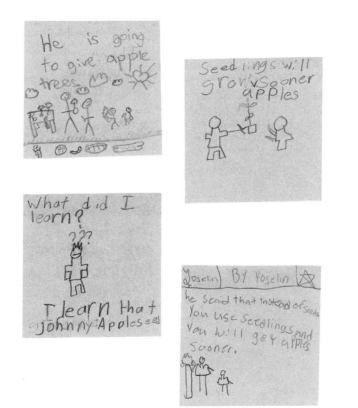

Sticky notes provide the perfect space for SASSy points.

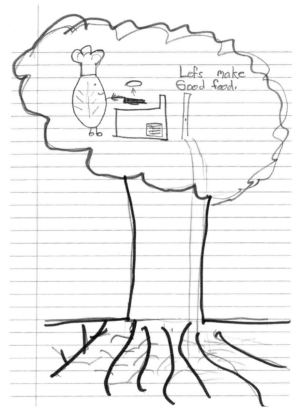

Independent sketch, completed by a student who truly did respond to opportunities to express herself in other than verbal means.

"MY VISUAL

Man

Woman

Astronaut

Doctor

well our brain is very intelligent and when you're proposing something you want to lear or be taught can achieve, this visual show the beginning and end of your achievement.

Thanks!!

Evidence of "change." He sketched this on the back of his paper. He wrote: "Well our brain is very intelligent and when you're proposing something you want to learn or be taught can achieve, this visual show the beginning and end of your achievement! Thanks!!" So, although he copied the sketchwork from an online site, he handily transferred that to his explanation.

Exercise your brain and you will be smarter!!

Learning about the brain and how it gets stronger in relation to use, this student asked to create a visual representation.

Thinking, or Copying?

Do my students copy my sketches? Sometimes yes. Sometimes no. When we are first starting out, they certainly do. Some students depend heavily on my ideas, and that's okay—I still hold them accountable to describe or explain the visual, either orally or in writing. It definitely quells anxiety, but it also sparks ideas. Many of my students will watch me draw first, then tweak it to make it their own. Some don't need my drawings to get started, but like to compare when they are done. Visualizing is a skill that needs to be taught. It's not easy, and many kids aren't used to imagining ideas concretely enough to transfer to paper. Give it time. Chances are, you'll do a bit of copying yourself as you discover your own edu-sketching groove.

Mirror Neurons

Speaking of copying, here's where mirror neurons come into play. In the 1990s a crew of Italian scientists were studying motor neurons when they discovered that certain neurons within a lab monkey fired when it performed an action.[11] Nothing earth-shattering. What surprised them was when they realized the same neurons fired in the monkey when it merely watched another monkey do the same thing. The neurons had, in a sense, adopted and mimicked the other being's mannerisms. This led researchers to believe, after further research, that these mirror neurons could be the basis behind our

unconscious imitation of others. Reading each other's intentions, each other's lips (as we unwittingly do), and even mimicking our conversational partner's mannerisms and posture are all testaments to this theory. V. S. Ramachandran, neuroscientist and author, calls some mirror neurons "'Gandhi cells' because they blur the boundary between self and others" when the neurons can't really tell the difference.[12]

Ramachandran considers mirror neurons "central to social learning, imitation, and the cultural transmission of skills and attitudes" thanks to the imitative learning associated with them.[13] So, as we consider building lessons, or parts of our lessons around visuals, keep in mind the role of these mirror neurons.

All that is to say that when our students watch us sketching and thinking aloud as we do so, their own brains are firing as if they, too, were doing the sketching.

OTHER TAKEAWAYS BASED ON MY EXPERIENCES

Drawing Faces

I generally don't draw faces. I subscribe to the "uncanny valley" theory. Masahiro Mori,[14] a robot designer, describes how we react to

---

11 Giacomo Rizzolatti and his colleagues, Giuseppe Di Pellegrino, Luciano Fadiga, and Vittorio Gallese, from the University of Parma, in Italy. Understanding motor events: A neurophysiological study. *Experimental Brain Research* (April 1992) 91: 176–180.

12 V. S. Ramachandran, *The Tell-Tale Brain* (New York: Norton, 2011).

13 Ibid., Kindle ed., location 628/6232.

14 M. Mori (June 2012). The Uncanny Valley. IEEE Spectrum. http://spectrum .ieee.org/automaton/robotics/humanoids/the-uncanny-valley. Also a good video explaining it: https://www.youtube.com/watch?v=aYuBDkto2Vk "What is the Uncanny Valley? Mashable Explains, June 2014.

robots and animated figures that appear to possess human characteristics. It turns out that the fewer human characteristics and details a figure has, the more readily acceptable it is by an audience. Apparently, more details increase recognition and familiarity, which in turn distract from meaning. Acceptance of the human-like character drops measurably, into a "valley" where its appearance is "uncanny," and becomes creepy to viewers, an effect found to be specifically related to human faces.

Our brains are supremely attuned to faces; evidence shows your brain is intriguingly more activated when watching or hearing another person, rather than a nonhuman mechanical robot, performing the same task.[15] It's because faces are such an important part of your world that your brain—pattern seeker extraordinaire that it is—is ready to see them everywhere, from the man in the moon to grilled cheese sandwiches.

So, along with this evidence, I know that my students get hung up on faces when I do add expressions (or try to). At times, it does distract them from the content; at other times, I will elicit ways of drawing how someone feels using other cues like hands on hips for anger or power, tears falling for sadness, sunshine for happiness, and so on. This can be done as a whole group, or it may be a question I ask an individual.

On the flip side, as Dan Roam notes, "People respond to people. Faces and stick figures, however crudely drawn, immediately elicit attention, understanding, and reaction."[16] I appreciate his recognition that the inherent imperfections of stick figures and basic drawings invite the audience to participate. I've experienced that myself, when my kids tell me to draw a happy face or make my stick figures "look mad"—and even to add speech or thought bubbles for emphasis. When this happens, I love to ask the students to come up to the board and add the details themselves.

Bottom line? I don't discourage my kids from drawing faces, but I've also discovered that not pushing them to do so alleviates a lot of anxiety around their sketches. Relying on other cues to distinguish your sketched characters also ramps up critical thinking skills. And again, the time factor comes in handy—providing 2 or 3 minutes for a quick sketch doesn't give them a lot of time for those teeny tiny details. They will learn to focus on the gist of the representations.

That being said, let your kids play for a bit and experiment. Have them draw circles and fill them in with different faces, just for fun, so that they have the tools. Play some music in the background and see if it makes a difference.

As you consider edu-sketching with your students, remember the four primary domains that we focus on in language learning: listening, speaking, reading, and writing. Each of these domains should be accessed by all students during any given class period, if possible. Edu-sketching, despite its seeming simplicity, does just that.

---

15 Lawrence Rosenblum, *See What I'm Saying* (New York: Norton, 2011), 176–179.

16 D. Roam (2008), The Lost Chapter from the Back of the Napkin. Accessed via Change This, Issue 44-03: http://changethis.com/manifesto/show/44.03.Ten Commandments; pdf file: http://www.principledinnovation.com/wp-content/uploads/2008/03/44.03.TenCommandments.pdf

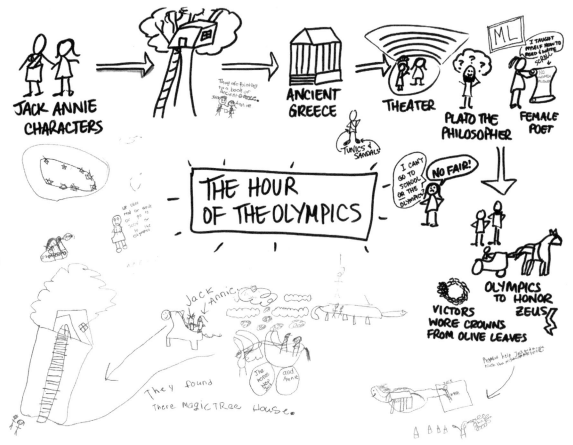

These shared images are visuals from the Magic Tree House, *Hour of the Olympics*. I sketched parts of it as we conducted retell of the story. They contributed orally, then they sketched the last couple of chapters.

next day actually helps them review. Ask them to add a new detail, color a fact that surprised them (from one of their sketches), or even just draw a circle, rectangle, or star around a word they learned.

Here are examples from when we learned about color usage as we read about Georgia O'Keeffe, and students began to understand how color can represent different feelings or emotions.

Color

When I sketch in class, I tend to use three or four colors at most. I steer away from lighter colors because kids can't see them. I also use the most common whiteboard marker colors if I'm sketching on the board.

On paper, I will also use only three or four colors, because I feel it can be distracting for the students otherwise. Sometimes I add more, but generally, in the interest of time and clarity, three or four.

Interestingly, my students don't often ask to color a sketch, unless it's a larger one. But even then, very few have done so. They seem to prefer the pencil and paper kind and, again, in the interest of saving time, it has been my go-to method.

Having kids return to their sketches and outline them in color the

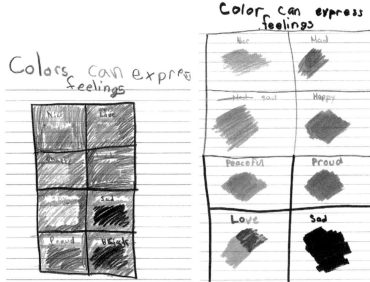

After reading about Georgia O'Keeffe, one of our sketches demonstrated colors we would use to represent certain emotions. This, in turn, led to a lot of fun discussion!

The greatest thing about edu-sketching is that there are so many options.

Spelling

I'm blessed with a spelling brain, but don't be a hater. As you may have noticed in some of my examples, my students still struggle with spelling, but you've got to make a decision about your objectives. Are you focusing on content? If so, the more important idea is communicability. Hang-ups about spelling can disrupt the flow of ideas, especially for struggling learners—they have so much to hold onto in their working memory that it's best sometimes just to let ideas pour out, grammar and spelling be damned.

If you're absolutely bent on ensuring perfect spelling, have students create their own word banks for a given topic, or if they keep getting stuck on certain words all the time (you know which ones those are—just take a look at commonly misspelled words), have them keep a mini notebook (i.e., portable) with the correct spellings for reference. Carrying a notebook, by the way, is also a great tactic for jotting down sketch ideas, notes, and other golden thoughts on the spot. (Yep, that whole memory deal—make friends with your memory. It gets by with a little help from its friends.)

Limits

Biz Stone, cofounder of Twitter, recounts a story about killing time drawing on the backs of place mats while waiting for his food to arrive at restaurants. He would ask his mom what to draw, and she would say, "Draw anything." Biz stared at his blank paper and repeated his question—"What should I draw?" Finally she'd tell him to draw a dump truck and he'd start drawing right away. He admits it was probably never even close to being a dump truck, but the takeaway is that limiting his options gave him a place to start. Constraints, counterintuitively, can enhance productivity and creativity. We do this with our questioning in class, right? Instead of saying, "How did you like that story? While students respond simply: It was good," we ask, "What do you think was the toughest part of making that decision for Character A?" Already the responses will be much more insightful—and yes, interesting.

Determining your SASSy points and crafting your questions are key. You might ask students how they would represent the main idea of a paragraph, or you might ask them to represent their prediction of what Character A saw when he peered out the window. Align your question with the intended outcome. Provide space for struggle, for multiple avenues of response. If you haven't noticed, sketching in class can be mentally challenging for teachers as well as students. It's not just "drawing in class"; these are pointed and deliberate ways to enhance thinking across the board.

Indeed, simple parameters like a folded page are useful—the predetermined stopping points allow you to choose the main ideas for students to represent. The time limit (typically 2 to 3 minutes per sketch) encourages them to sketch quickly without worrying too much about serious detail or perfectionism, and the smaller space is far less intimidating—students don't feel like they have to fill up some massive white space.

It's also helpful to use these folded divisions for separate topics. In this example, we were learning about four different genres, and the students compiled their notes in five boxes. We began with the center box together—defining what the four genres had in common (old stories and created for both children and adults).

Students were grouped for a jigsaw activity; each of the four groups worked with their partners to come up with visuals and characteristics for their respective genre. They then shared with the the the rest of the class. As they shared, they explained the thinking behind their sketches, and the others could copy their sketches. (Talk about excited kids to see their ideas re-created by the others.)

Students can share their favorite sketch at the end—with a partner or the group. The boxes also allow students to create a sequenced written summary. Have them go back and write a single sentence about each sketch or box the next day; doing so helps them cement their recall of details. These sentences can then be combined to create a written summary in paragraph form while they're being encouraged (coerced?) to revisit sketches and clarify what they were thinking.

I loved her use of the gear wheels to represent the concept of myths imparting how the world works.

You can see how students can bring what resonates most into their sketches, at least as a baseline. Fairytales here have talking animals, a giant, fairies, and someone carrying treasure.

This student copied from student A (America), after she explained her sketching idea and understanding.

It's expected that students understand and analyze political cartoons, but having them actually generate them, with the nuances and just enough detail to leave space for inferencing, brings the intellectual challenge to new heights. Here, this student represented "the CDC saying it has Ebola under control when it really doesn't. It's irony because the CDC is standing over a dead pile of people. They don't have it under control or have a good cure for it. The US is send it US Millitary to help. The US military might get ebola."

The CDC saying it has ebola under contoral when it really doesn't. It's irony because the CDC is standing over a dead pile of people. They don't have it under contoral or have a good cure for it. The U.S is send it U.S military to help. The U.S military might get ebola.

Political Cartoons

Students are required to analyze political cartoons, but what happens to their thinking when asked to create one? Depicting irony and then describing in writing how it pokes fun at particular governmental agencies is a tall order for any thinker. Having never been asked to do that before, my students claimed it hurt their brains to actually create one themselves. The drawings may not be as detailed as a professional's, but it was the first time I'd tried it with students, and I'll definitely try it again.

Students Who Are Reluctant to Draw

Yep. You will have students who are reluctant to draw. My theory on that is to let it go. As long as they are still taking notes and keeping pace with the content, I've never found it useful to force students to sketch. Often, I will encourage them with a topic I know they're interested in, or partner them up to create a joint sketch. I've got to say that even though I've had a couple (very few) reluctant students, every single one of them eventually created some sketches. As you've seen in my examples, sketching does not need to be elaborate, large, or public. On the contrary, it can be something purely private and personal—and that knowledge helps staunch resistance.

Assessment

(Because what educational book would be complete without it?)

Edu-sketching is what I consider an inherently formative assessment tool, and I've mentioned myriad ways to incorporate it into

No matter how you dress 'em up, those formal tests still loom large.

A.K.A.- THE FORMAL TEST

your classroom instruction. It can also be part of a summative assessment, or a more formal formative assessment.

This type of assessment, as you've read repeatedly, encourages visual, tactile, and kinesthetic learners to maximize their expressive strengths. Gauge the amount of time for students to spend on a sketch based on whether you want to use it as a formative or summative assessment—then allow appropriate time for written explanation. It's helpful, too, if you plan on edu-sketching for summative assessments, to analyze elements of a good visual and what's lacking in one that needs a little work. Models for your students are extremely helpful, even if you think they will copy. They will, but they will also delight you with their own talents.

Ask for summaries with a detailed sketch, labeled with phrases or specific academic content vocabulary, then a written summary (or not). Although summaries usually involve writing, this encourages thinking first and reflecting as students draw, before writing. Some students just work better this way. It's up to you if you want to add the paragraph or essay writing as support. These are just options.

Differentiate the process according to ability. Vary the number of details, divide the paper into predetermined parts or sizes, and establish SASSy points in the text if need be. If students are reading a particularly dense text, consider providing guided notes with spaces for well-timed sketches.

Creating a rubric will save you many headaches, and it can be simple. Use it to delineate desired characteristics such as labels, phrases, sentences, or key vocabulary. Maybe your focus is on structure or order—include organization for aspects like a flowchart, indicated sequence, or paragraph that fully explains the content depicted. Maybe you're seeking evidence of even deeper understanding: include areas appropriate for irony or inferences. You can also include an oral proficiency rubric if you want students to present an oral description. You can also ask them to describe elements of a good visual, particularly sketched representations—what is useful for them, time limits, minimal levels of content information provided, and so on. Getting students involved in as many aspects of their learning as possible deepens their metacognitive awareness. And that, my friends, makes for a very happy brain.

Metacognition and Reflection

Make sure sketching is not just an activity. For the most benefit, after your students create visuals (particularly after the first few times), have students respond explicitly to questions like these, either orally, or in writing:

1. What did we do today (or the past few days)?
2. What was the purpose of this (type of) lesson?
3. How did this skill (or lesson) help you meet the learning objectives?
4. How did today's learning build on what you already know and are able to do?
5. How will this lesson help you in the future?

As teachers, we must understand that a neural pathway is like a new path in the woods. The more frequently a neural pathway is traveled, the fewer the obstacles, the greater its capacity, and the smoother and faster it becomes.

We can help our students connect to prior experiences, knowledge, and learning—and to other curricular areas—through edusketching, as it helps us connect with students and shape our instruction to their understanding. It promotes the strengthening of neural pathways and more memorable learning because the pieces become part of a greater whole.

Knowing this, it becomes all the more crucial to maximize learning opportunities during the 1,260 hours our students are with us during the school year.[17] Studies show that we as teachers spend 90% of planning time ensuring our lessons make sense. We tend to spend far less planning time (about 10%) on establishing the relevance of the lesson to previous and future learning, despite neuroscientific findings that indicate relevance—linked to connections and emotion—is particularly important.[18]

Students benefit most from doing the work, from generating thought, and from expressing their thinking in ever clearer ways. That includes productive speaking, active and intentional listening, close reading, and detailed writing. All of these promote deeper thinking and, with edu-sketching, a safe space to do so. Reflection, synthesis, evaluation, and knowledge combine to create a unique learning and remembering experience. Use it when you want to test the depth of their knowledge, tap into their nonverbal expression skills, or need a novel change of pace. Any way you look at it, you will uncover insights into your students' knowledge that otherwise may have been stashed away for good.

Judy Willis talks of the timely convergence of neuroscience and education during this creativity crisis, in which the arts are being displaced by more standardized and testable subject areas.[19] What we call higher-order thinking or critical thinking, neuroscientists call executive function. Whatever your moniker, it's a holy grail of sorts for the cognitive push we want to give our students.

Try edu-sketching for yourself, and you will find that many of those skills are covered with the use of a simple, humble sketch. Critical analysis, using prior knowledge to make predictions (not just activating it), inducting and deducting, symbolic conceptualization, and using prior knowledge to support learning or create something new are all executive functions that come into play with creative thinking processes. Maybe edu-sketching is the way to make those direct correlations that we educators are starting to seek between the neuroscience research and our classrooms.

Twenty-first-century skills, exemplified through pencil and paper. How ironic is that?

---

17 "Beyond PISA: How the United States Compares With High-Achieving Nations on Key Educational Issues," NEA Research, June 2013, http://neatoday.org/wp-content/uploads/2013/06/US-InternationalComparisons.pdf.

18 Wendi Pillars, "Teachers as Brain-Changers," *Education Week*, December 20, 2011.

19 J. Willis, http://www.teachthought.com/learning/the-impact-of-creativity-on-the-brain/ (2013).

CHAPTER FIVE: IN A NUTSHELL

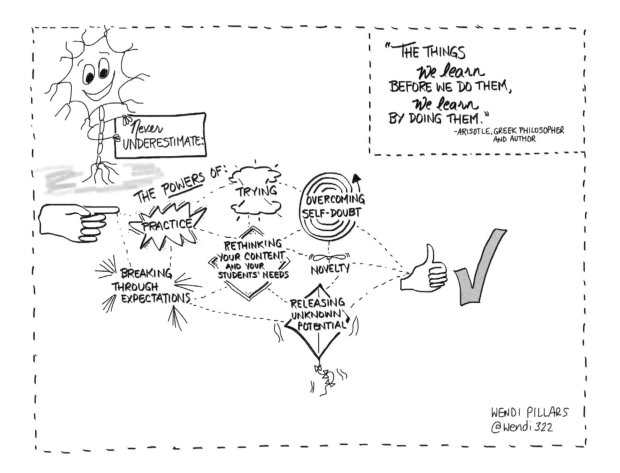

The things we have to learn before we do them, we learn by doing them.   —*Aristotle, Greek philosopher and author*

Although this marks the conclusion of this book, it signals the start of your journey to take the nuggets that apply to you, polish them with your own panache, and implement them liberally in your classroom.

As you've surmised by now, this book is more of a teaching tool than a how-to manual of teaching. There is simply no way to wave a magic wand and reduce the complex art of teaching down to a strategy or two, but edu-sketching can be a powerful process and tool for any teacher to include in their repertoire.

Along with providing opportunities for our students to think in new ways and to express their knowledge through a variety of outlets, it is critical for us to pass along information about how their brains actually learn. Doing so can help students optimize their learning experiences or at least help them make more sense of those experiences. Along with learning about our brains, students will relish the stories of people with marvelously different thought processes, the ones who highlight that it's more than okay to think differently and to express knowledge in non-standardized ways.

The outward simplicity of edu-sketching belies its mental workout and power. Real thought and creativity are required, and it takes practice to open your mind's eye. This is one of those teaching strategies that, in the words of Aristotle, you must do yourself to feel its impact, as the exercises included in the book are intended to demonstrate.

As you embark on your edu-sketching journey with your beloved students, remember these few ideas:

- Try one step at a time, then build upon it with your students because this approach involves them wholly and directly.
- Find and use materials that are especially adept at evoking images, in order to see things through different lenses and to get ideas.
- Find examples of metaphor-rich language and concepts, from the concrete to the more abstract, then sit with them to understand their power.
- Become one with the idea that less is more—edu-sketching narrows our focus and trims the excess verbal fluff with which we tend to pad our content.
- Take the chance even if you think you can't. (Yes, you can draw.)
- Have fun.
- And practice.

There, within edu-sketching, my friends, is your secret sauce—the kind that can make a lesson you already have that much tastier and more memorable. Earth-shattering? Nope. But it is a spoonful of yum to make your students come back for more as they deepen their learning.

In the words of David Hockney, "Drawing makes you see things clearer, and clearer, and clearer still. The image is passing through you in a physiological way, into your brain, into your memory—where it stays—it's transmitted by your hands."[20] And that, dear edu-sketchers, is a gift. Grow, dendrites, grow.

---

20 Grayford, M. (Sept. 2011). The many layers of David Hockney. *The Telegraph*. http://www.telegraph.co.uk/culture/art/art-features/8782275/The-many-layers-of-David-Hockney.html

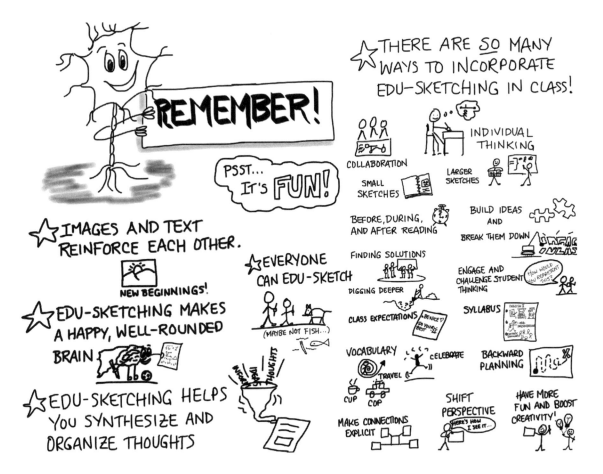

Brain-Imaging Techniques

electroencephalography (EEG). Measures brain waves, the electrical patterns created by the rhythmic oscillations of neurons. These waves are characterized according to the type of brain activity occurring, and the EEG measures these waves by picking up signals via electrodes placed in the skull. The latest version of EEG takes readings from multiple spots and compares them, resulting in a picture of activity across the brain. Brain mapping with EEG sometimes uses event-related potentials, which simply means that an electric peak (potential) is related to a particular stimulus, such as a word or a touch.

functional MRI (fMRI). Elaborates the basic image from MRIs by adding the areas of greatest activity in the brain. Neuronal firing is fueled by glucose and oxygen, which are transported by the blood. When an area of the brain is activated, the glucose and oxygen flow toward it, and fMRI shows the location of high amounts of oxygen. This is a rapid scanning technique (about four images per second); the brain takes about half a second to react to a stimulus, so fMRI can show the flow of activity during a reaction. It is one of the more telling and rewarding of the techniques, but cost-prohibitive. Hence, other, older methods are more often used.

magnetic resonance imaging (MRI). Sometimes called nuclear magnetic resonance imaging (NMRI),[1] MRI works by aligning atomic particles in the body tissues via magnetism, then bombarding them with radio waves. This causes the particles to emit radio signals that differ according to what sort of tissue is present. Software known as computerized tomography converts this information into a three-dimensional picture of any part of the body. A brain scan taken with MRI looks like a grayish X-ray, with different, clearly delineated types of tissue.

magnetoencephalography (MEG). Is similar to EEG in that it picks up oscillation signals, but it does so by honing in on the tiny magnetic pulse emitted rather than the electric field. The drawback is that signals tend to be weak and subject to interference, but its enormous potential rests in the fact that it is faster than other scanning techniques and can even chart changes in brain activity more accurately than fMRI or PET.

multimodal Imaging. Increasingly popular, and combines two or more of these techniques to give a more complete picture.

near-infrared spectroscopy (NIRS). Also produces images based on the amount of fuel needed at any given moment by each area of the brain during an activity. It works by beaming low-level light waves into the brain and measuring the varying amount reflected from each area. NIRS is cheaper than fMRI, plus does not use radioactiv-

---

1 Information for this appendix is taken primarily from R. Carter, *Mapping the Mind* (London: Weidenfeld and Nicolson, 1998); S. Greenfield, *The Human Mind Explained* (New York: Henry Holt, 1996); and Wikipedia.

ity, but it cannot provide a clear picture of activity in deeper regions in the brain.

positron emission tomography (PET). Results of PET are similar to fMRI in that it identifies the hardest-working areas of the brain by measuring their glucose and oxygen fuel intakes. The pictures produced are known for their clarity, but cannot achieve the higher resolution of fMRI. The drawback of PET is its required injection of a radioactive marker into the bloodstream; because of this injection—albeit tiny—scanning sessions are limited to one annually.

Cellular Phases During Development

Some important developmental processes in the brain include the following.

cell death. In the normal course of CNS development, nerve cells are pruned away. Apparently, the cells are removed aggressively and efficiently in order to leave optimum numbers of stronger and well-connected neurons.

cell migration. Neurons may travel from their place of origin to their final positions in the nervous system. Cells in the cerebral cortex, for example, may move from the inner surface of the neural tube to the outer surface—a substantial distance in cellular terms. Migration occurs more in waves, rather than at a constant rate, and these waves correlate with different cell types. Most migration occurs early in gestation, when the distances are smaller, but longer cell migrations within the cerebral cortex, hippocampus, and cerebellum continue well into the first year of life. Glial cells are helpful during migration.

myelination. Axons are coated, or insulated, by sheets of glial tissue that form the myelin sheath. This allows for more rapid signal transmission along the axon. Myelination is a continual process, with new waves being formed well into adulthood.

neuron proliferation. Even before the neural tube closes, neurons are being formed. The generation of these cells continues throughout gestation and well into the first year of life. Nuclear groups in the brain stem tend to form earlier than complex layered structures like the cerebral cortex, hippocampus, and cerebellum—which add cells over a longer period of time. Many structures within the central nervous system (CNS) produce neurons in excess of what is needed, so the proliferation period is followed by a period of cell death (apoptosis) to trim down the final number of neurons.

Cell proliferation occurs everywhere in the body, yet CNS cells are more sensitive than cells of other organs. Other organ systems develop differently than the CNS; the CNS is characterized by its continual addition of new cell types—dozens of different types—whereas other organ systems acquire basic cells, then increase numbers of these cells.

synaptogenesis. Proper connections must be achieved in order for neurons to function as transmitters of signals, so specialized structures must form on the surfaces of sending and receiving neurons. Recall that the point of connection is the synapse. Typically, neurons are covered with thousands of synapses, with receptor cells appearing on similar cells. Neurons maintain the capacity to create new synapses throughout life, but the developmental period is critical in the formation of the nervous system's foundational circuitry.

W. Pillars, "Mind the (Synaptic) Gap," master's thesis, Department of Peace Studies, University of Bradford, United Kingdom, 2004.

Content Area Sketches

Examples of sketch starters for different content areas, vocabulary, or even grammar points—what can you, readers, add? What are some key symbols and elements that thread through your content area? What are some unique symbols? How can you create them quickly, and tweak them to suit your style?

SOCIAL STUDIES

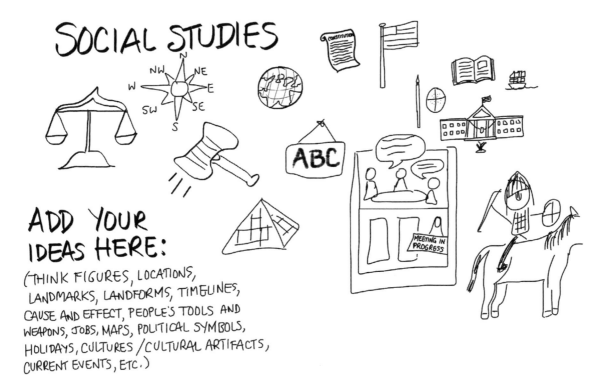

ADD YOUR IDEAS HERE:

(THINK FIGURES, LOCATIONS,
LANDMARKS, LANDFORMS, TIMELINES,
CAUSE AND EFFECT, PEOPLE'S TOOLS AND
WEAPONS, JOBS, MAPS, POLITICAL SYMBOLS,
HOLIDAYS, CULTURES / CULTURAL ARTIFACTS,
CURRENT EVENTS, ETC.)

...AND SO MANY MORE!